AUSTRALIAN STORIES For the Heart

AUSTRALIAN STORIES
For the Heart

STRAND PUBLISHING
Sydney

Australian Stories for the Heart
Copyright © 2002 by Strand Publishing
Copyright of the individual stories remains the property of the contributors

First published 2002 by Strand Publishing

ISBN: 187 682 509X

Distributed in Australia by:
Family Reading Publications
B100 Ring Road
Ballarat Victoria 3352
Phone: 03 5334 3244
Fax: 03 5334 3299
Email: info@familyreading.com.au

Unless otherwise noted, Scripture quotations are taken from *The Holy Bible, New International Version*®. Copyright © 1973, 1978, 1984 by International Bible Society. Used by permission of Zondervan. All rights reserved.
Quotations marked AMP are taken from *The Amplified*® *Bible*. Copyright © 1954, 1958, 1962, 1964, 1965, 1987 by The Lockman Foundation. Used by permission. (www.Lockman.org)
Quotations marked CEV are taken from *The Holy Bible: Contemporary English Version*, Copyright © American Bible Society, 1995.
Quotations marked NASB are taken from *The New American Standard Bible*®. Copyright © 1960, 1962, 1963, 1968, 1971, 1972, 1973, 1975, 1977, 1995 by The Lockman Foundation. Used by permission. (www.Lockman.org)
Quotations marked NKJV are taken from the *The Holy Bible, New King James Version*. Copyright © 1982 by Thomas Nelson, Inc. Used by permission. All rights reserved.
Quotations marked TEV are taken from *The Good News Bible: Today's English Version*. Copyright © American Bible Society, 1992. Used by permission. All rights reserved.
Quotations marked THE MESSAGE are taken from *The Message* by Eugene H. Peterson, Copyright © 1993, 1994, 1995, 1996, 2000. Used by permission of NavPress Publishing Group. All rights reserved.

This book is copyright. No part of this publication may be reproduced except for brief quotations in reviews without the prior permission of the publisher.

Cover photography courtesy of Ken Duncan Australia Wide Pty Ltd,
Copyright © Ken Duncan

Compiled by David and Rachel Dixon
Edited by Owen Salter
Cover design by Joy Lankshear
Typeset by Midland Typesetters, Maryborough, Victoria
Printed by Griffin Press, Netley, South Australia

Contents

Mountain-Moving Faith *Gordon Moyes* 1
Skin Deep Fear *Max Meyers* 4
In the Heart of Afghanistan's Suffering *Diana Thomas* 9
How Much for the Artificial Legs? *Colin Buchanan* 15
Attitude Makes the Difference *Philip Baker* 19
The Little Things *Warwick Saxby* 21
Miracle in Capernaum *Geoff Bullock* 25
A Tale of Two Pubs *Michael Frost* 31
I'm Rich! *Grenville Kent* 35
The Power of Praise *Darlene Zschech* 38
Giving out of Poverty *Amanda Smith* 41
More Beyond *Gordon Moyes* 43
Aced by Despair *Margaret Court and Barbara Oldfield* 46
Meeting the Megastar *John Dickson* 50
September Agent *Irene Voysey* 53
Fair Dinkum with God *Kel Richards* 57
Come Home *Brian Pickering* 60
Lesson in a Petrol Station *Kim Hawtrey* 64
Finding God in the Mud *Michael Frost* 67
The Strangest Gift *Phillip Jensen* 70
Big Plan *Angela Eynaud* 73
Rita and Evonne *Dave Andrews* 76

Lego and Life *Kim Hawtrey* 83
Doughnuts *Philip Baker* 86
God As Business Partner *Gordon Moyes* 88
A Canticle for Catherine *Sue Duggan* 91
Narrabeen's Story *Mal Garvin* 96
The Idol Busyness of Suburbia *Phillip Jensen* 100
Destination: Anywhere *Colin Buchanan* 103
The Party Dress *Angela Eynaud* 107
Neil's Spiritual U-turn *Philip Johnson* 110
The Widow's Mite *Jonathan Krause* 116
Photos, Faith and Finances *Steve Grace* 119
Doubts *Max Meyers* 124
Does God Watch Football? *Nathan Brown* 132
Signposts *Ken Duncan* 135
The Devil Pushed Me *Fred Nile* 138
A Church with Sole *Michael Frost* 143
The Squatter and the Swaggie *Kel Richards* 146
Radio Saved Her Life *Gordon Moyes* 151
Living for Tomorrow *Amanda Smith* 157
God's Improbable Choices *John Mallison* 160
A Small Butterfly *Margaret Reeson* 163
The Unseen Hand *Dudley Foord* 168
It's Raining Men *Darlene Zschech* 170
The Not-Sure Syndrome *Kim Hawtrey* 171
The Heart of O'Doherty *Irene Voysey* 174
Never, Never Give Up *Dudley Foord* 178
Answers to Prayer *Brian Pickering* 180
The Gates of Hell *Geoff Bullock* 184

Australian Stories for the Heart

Grace-Filled Living *Michael Frost* 189
The Real Thing *Angela Eynaud* 191
The Girl Who Was Always Ahead *David R. Nicholas* 195
Stranger Than Fiction *John Dickson* 197
Removing the *Jody V Millennium Michael Frost* 204
No Swimming! *Ken Duncan* 208
The Back of Bourke *Colin Buchanan* 209
Breakfast and Blessing *Darlene Zschech* 212
Overcoming Entropy *Amanda Smith* 215
The Day Christ Stopped the Bulldozers *Dave Andrews* 217
Hedonists Don't Get No Satisfaction *Grenville Kent* 224
The Truth Versus the Facts *Christine Caine* 229
God in the Strip Club *Michael Frost* 232
My Escape from the World Trade Centre *Hans Kunnen* 236
Meeting the Godfather *Grenville Kent* 242

Contributors 245
Credits 256

Mountain-Moving Faith

Gordon Moyes

What mountain are you facing? Australians know much about moving mountains. We have shifted Mount Tom Price, Iron Knob, Mount Hamersley, Mount Isa, the Snowy Mountains and Broken Hill. We can shift mountains by using heavy machinery. But how can you shift mountains by faith?

With faith you require only two things: work and persistence!

I had to shift a hill once. In 1972 my wife and I purchased an elevated one-storey house. I decided to turn it into a two-storey house. As I could not lift it up, I decided to go down. The house was 45 feet long and 25 feet wide. We had to go down about four to six feet. There was not enough room under the house for a machine so it had to be done with a shovel.

I said to the mountain of earth, 'Move from here to there!' The Lord said to me, 'Get a pick, a shovel and a wheelbarrow.'

I got under the house and started digging. I filled up a wheelbarrow and wheeled it to the front. We had half an acre of land on a gentle hill, so I started building up the bottom of the hill. Then another barrow. And another. Then fifty. Every Monday for months, with a pick, a shovel and a barrow, I said to the Lord, 'Move this mountain!' and the Lord said, 'Wheel the barrow!'

Gradually I began to see a hole under the house. It was then I discovered a second great truth about dirt. More comes out of a hole than was in there originally. A hundred barrows of earth levelled the front lawn. Two hundred barrows of earth meant that the block beside us was now level. Meanwhile, we had to bring in truckloads of sand and metal. I mixed and barrowed hundreds of loads of concrete.

Then I fitted in new house stumps and a huge steel beam under the floor. I installed a dozen windows and built dividing walls. In went the first rumpus room, then the laundry. Through the earth moving the house began to grow. After two years I had shifted enough earth to add a garage and workshop. I kept saying to the Lord, 'Move this mountain,' and the Lord replied each time, 'Keep wheeling. You and I are in this together.' (I said, 'Yes, Lord, but I'm the one who's getting hot!')

Slowly the front lawn area became smooth. Then came more concrete and finally the big, double rumpus room. Seven years after I began digging, the hill was at last removed.

We finished the walls. We put up the table-tennis table. The furniture was in and the carpet was down, and we had a house double its original size and triple its value. Everything was beautiful.

Then, just as I finished, Wesley Mission said, 'Come to Sydney!'

When we put our Victorian home on the market, an interested purchaser said, 'What a lovely front lawn you have!' He didn't know that faith, plus work, plus persistence had doubled the size of a house and turned a hill into a smooth lawn.

You can shift mountains from here to there with faith and persistent work. These were the words of Jesus: 'If you have faith as small as a mustard seed, you can say to this mountain, "Move from here to there" and it will move. Nothing will be impossible for you' (Matthew 17:20). That is his promise.

I believe that what the mind can conceive and the heart can believe, the will can achieve. All things are possible to those who have faith. If you don't think something is possible, you will be right. But if you think it *is* possible, you will be right! Only faith achieves.

Skin Deep Fear

Max Meyers

These were not ordinary passengers, these four Samberigi men.

Brown skinned and muscular, they were mountain men of Papua New Guinea's southern highlands. But on this day they exhibited none of the strength and confidence that would mark them as warriors who should be taken seriously. They carried no weapons.

They were sick and needed treatment. The small mission clinic at Samberigi was insufficient, and knowing that I was planning to fly across the mountains to the north coast, the station nurse asked me to drop these men off along the way. Mendi, about twenty minutes flying to the northwest, had a regional hospital.

As I fastened their seatbelts, I explained as best I could what they should expect on this short flight. But they appeared very uneasy. This was to be their first flight ever. Even for the initiated, flying in Papua New Guinea is often a daunting experience. To these tribesmen, who had grown up in the Stone Age, it may be nothing short of terrifying. I noticed the deteriorating weather and thought it could be a daunting experience for me!

Soon after takeoff, light rain began to paint its peculiar patterns on the windshield. Earlier, on the way up from Wasua, my home base on the Fly River, the weather had been reasonably good. At least at a higher altitude. But now the clouds grew ominous atop the mountain peaks. If I climbed above them, it would be difficult to find a way down again. Particularly in the relatively confined space of the Mendi valley.

I headed northwest, tracing the winding path of the mighty Erave River gorge. To the left and to the right majestic peaks filled the sky. On a clear day this steep gorge would present a vista of great beauty. Today, the light was a diffused grey, the river white and turbulent. Misty rain, whipped by mountains winds, produced a strange, matted effect upon the valley walls, and the higher ridges were enshrouded in cloud. From the cockpit of my Cessna it almost seemed as if I was flying into the throat of a very inhospitable grey tunnel.

I noticed a narrow space between the cloud and the ridge to my right and made a quick turn into the next valley with the wheels of the aircraft almost touching the ridge top. I flew east along that valley, planning to regain my track farther up. Thus, in a zigzag fashion, valley by valley, I made my way toward Mendi.

For a while I wondered whether I would find Mendi at all. I wished that I had not agreed to make this diversion. It would have been simple to fly to the south out of Samberigi for a few miles to climb above the clouds, then to negotiate a way through the mountains to Wewak, my final destination.

Totally absorbed as the minutes ticked by, I paid no attention to my passengers. Suddenly I heard a sound coming from the backseat. It was a low, drawn-out moan! I turned back.

There in the backseat, locked together in an embrace of abject fear, were my three mountain men. Their three black, curly heads were close together, their faces beaded with perspiration. Three pairs of arms were locked together. And staring back at me, three terror-filled pairs of eyes. They were speechless with fear. And my faltering words of encouragement did little to comfort them.

If this flight's tough for me, how must they be feeling? I thought.

I glanced across to check on my fourth passenger, sitting in the front seat. He, however, had a completely different demeanour. I was surprised. He was staring ahead, contemplative and detached. Even casual.

'Yu no gat pret?' I asked him. ('Aren't you afraid?')

He turned and looked squarely into my eyes. His response was slow and deliberate. I think he'd asked himself the same question.

'Skin bilong mi tasol I pret.' ('Only my skin is afraid.')

What? Only his skin?

I talked on.

'So only your skin is afraid?' I asked. 'What about the rest of you?'

Pointing out of the window, he answered in his pidgin English with one of the most expressive and profound statements I have ever heard.

'I see the mountains,' he said. 'They are so close.' He gestured with a wave of his hand.

'I see the trees and the rocks as they rush by. I see the rain, and I hear it beating on the glass. I see the clouds all around us. All I see brings fear to me. I didn't know that this big bird of yours shook like this as it flew along. There is much to be afraid of here.'

Then with a smile he continued, 'But my fear is only as deep as my skin.'

'What about the rest of you?' I asked again. 'What about under your skin?'

'I am not afraid under my skin,' he said. 'You see, I know the One who made the mountains. I know the One who made the rocks and the trees. I know the One who made the clouds and the rain for today. He has told me that I don't need to be afraid. Why? Because he lives in me. Inside my skin. And he has promised never to leave me. Because of that, I am not afraid.'

He smiled at me. I grinned back at him, incredulous. What a fantastic 'show and tell' of true, heaven-sent faith.

Fear was understandable in this situation. It was absolutely consuming his three friends in the back seat. But not him.

Fear was not granted entry beneath his skin. God was there.

In the Heart of Afghanistan's Suffering

Diana Thomas

More than twenty years of war and three years of drought had taken their toll on the Afghan people. They had fought a Soviet invasion and communist rule, and had then fallen victim to the extremist Taliban regime, which prided itself on being the purest Islamic country in the world.

Many Afghans languished in prisons for minor infringements under the Taliban, for 'crimes' such as running away from a cruel husband or answering a doorbell without wearing a burqa. Music and dancing were outlawed, girls and women denied employment and education. Public executions and chopping off of hands took place regularly in the sports stadium in Kabul. The Taliban had taken Afghanistan back to the dark ages.

On August 3, 2001, two of our Shelter Now team members were arrested when they visited an Afghan family in Kabul they had befriended. We later realised that the visit was a set up by the family. The remaining six of us were arrested in our houses or office. It would be almost two months before we would find out what our charges were. In all, twenty-four of us were imprisoned—sixteen Afghan workers and eight foreign workers.

Shortly after our capture, we decided to have meetings twice a day to praise and worship God and to pray. It wasn't long before we understood we had a mission. God gave us this verse of Scripture: 'Seek the peace and prosperity of the city to which I have carried you into exile. Pray to the Lord for it, because if it prospers, you too will prosper' (Jeremiah 29:7).

We believed we had been handpicked by God to intercede for Afghanistan. The Taliban had intended to harm us, but God intended to use us to save many lives (Genesis 50:20). There is a price to pay for saving many lives; for Joseph it was many years in obscurity, enduring injustice. For us it was to be in Kabul in a time of war with bombs falling all around us.

After the September 11 attack on the United States, all foreigners in Afghanistan were evacuated—except for us. We were prisoners of Jesus Christ, and God put us in the heart of Afghanistan's suffering so that we could pray. While in the prison, the Lord gave Scriptures to us: 'I will not die but live, and will proclaim what the Lord has done' (Psalm 118:17); 'He ransoms me unharmed from the battle waged against me, even though many oppose me' (Psalm 55:18). We also clung to Psalm 91 and Psalm 124: 'If the Lord had not been on our side . . . they would have swallowed us alive . . . We have escaped like a bird out of the fowler's snare . . .' The Lord gave melodies to the ladies to which we sang passages of Scripture.

Almost every word in the Bible dealing with trials and persecutions took on a new meaning for me. My hardest test was my willingness to lose our house and all of my belongings. After three days of inner turmoil, I gave all to him. We can truly trust him with our lives and with everything we own.

Many times we sang, 'God is good all the time.' I came to a place of really believing this. I can say with all assurance that God is good, not just some of the time, but *all* of the time. One of our ladies saw angels with their arms interlocked all around the compound where we were.

Unusual noise and activity on the night of November 14 led us to believe that something was going to happen. Georg Taubmann, a German aid worker with Shelter Now, came up to see us on the pretence that he needed some medicine from us. 'There are radio reports that the Northern Alliance is only 10 kilometres out of Kabul,' he said. 'Something may happen tonight, but don't open your door unless you hear my voice.'

At about 10:30 p.m., the Taliban came knocking on our doors but we waited until we heard the voices of Georg and Peter Bunch before we came out (Peter was the other imprisoned Australian aid worker). The Taliban tried to hurry us, telling us to leave our stuff in the room and promising we would return later, but we took everything. They wanted to put us into two vehicles, but I told Georg I wanted us all to travel in one. So all eight of us squashed into one vehicle. One side of the seat had rocket launchers and we had to sit on top of them.

We sang songs of praise, and Heather Mercer read Scriptures out to us under torchlight as we headed down the road to Kandahar. We saw many Taliban fleeing towards their militia stronghold in Kandahar with rocket launchers in the back of their pickup vehicles.

Half way between Kabul and Ghazni, our captors said that they wanted money for our release. A few hours later, guards stopped the vehicle and told us we would have to sleep in a shipping container, one of many that lined the road. It was a freezing night and our feet were like ice blocks; we had to huddle together to keep warm.

Early in the morning we continued on to Ghazni where we were put in a prison worse than any we had experienced in Kabul. There was no running water and the toilet was so blocked that the excrement was piling up. Our captors were searching for a satellite phone to ring our embassies, hoping to acquire a ransom of $5 million for our release.

As soon as we entered the prison, America started bombing and firing on the city of Ghazni. The building shook and we felt unsafe because we knew the Americans didn't realise we were there.

We started worshipping and praying, sensing God's wonderful peace over the next one and a half hours. Suddenly we heard someone trying to break into the prison. Then wild-looking men burst into our room with rocket launchers and Kalashnikovs in their hands. They told us that we were free and that the Taliban had gone. We were amazed and excited!

After the bombing stopped, we rushed out into the streets where people were celebrating and rejoicing. Women waved to us from their gates, no longer wearing burqas covering their faces.

We later learned that 200 Arab terrorists had fled Ghazni before we entered the city. While we were worshipping and praying in prison, there was so much confusion amongst the Taliban that they fought each other before finally fleeing the city.

The situation was still not safe in Ghazni. The next day was frustrating as Georg sought assistance and cooperation from a local area commander and the Red Cross to take us to an airport where the Americans had planned to pick us up at around midnight. In the meantime, the owner of the house we were staying in was starting to feel very anxious about our presence in his house, in case the Taliban returned or trouble arose.

At 10.30 p.m., Georg convinced the local area commander to take us to a disused airstrip not far from the house. Leaving with only what we had on, we walked fifteen minutes in the dark to the airstrip. After waiting for about two hours, we were rescued by the American Special Forces in military helicopters.

Only God could have designed it so that his people would still be in Afghanistan to intercede for the nation in a time of war. Since our release, we have learned that millions of Christians were burdened to pray for our safety and release.

What was so amazing to us was that God took us out of Kabul an hour before that city fell into the hands of the Northern Alliance. We had also prayed that our sixteen Afghan workers would be released before us, and that this would be a sign that we too would be set free. They were released a day before us. God showed us that we could not trust in the lawyer, judge, diplomats and others who wanted to help us; he wanted us to trust only in him.

Our God is an awesome God! To him be all the glory!

Afghanistan required much prayer before God could move his mighty hand over that nation to break the curse of all the innocent blood that has been shed there. I believe that our capture, especially after September 11, prompted millions of people to pray for Afghanistan. God removed a wicked regime so that many may enter his kingdom.

How Much for the Artificial Legs?

Colin Buchanan

Can't resist a junk shop. Especially a junk shop in the bush. Old wares, bric-a-brac, second-hand treasure—love it! Got my radar turned on every time I drive into a new town. Stuff piled on the footpath, maybe a yard out the back with rusting, decaying items with slim potential commercial value. Lock in, pull up, groans and protestations from travelling companions (kids, wife, family, musicians etc.). But I am a man on a mission. I have sighted a junk shop and I must browse.

But be warned. Disappointments await the junk shop junkie who lacks discernment. Fallen for some of these myself, so pay close attention. Perhaps cut this section out and pop it on the fridge. Commit it to memory. It will serve you well in the search for T.U.J.S. (The Ultimate Junk Shop).

A craft shop IS NOT A JUNK SHOP. A shop that sells jams with little bits of material stretched over the lids and held on with a rubber band IS NOT A JUNK SHOP. If the sign says

'Antiques' and it has lockable glass cabinets, halogen down lights and the proprietor wears a scarf, IT IS NOT A JUNK SHOP. Anywhere that provides an outlet for local artists and potters IS NOT A JUNK SHOP. If their stock consists of more than 30 per cent of any of the following:
- woollen products (knitted, crocheted or woven)
- honey
- wooden toys
- resort wear
- things that have been stuffed (animals excluded)
- dried flowers
- folk art

IT IS NOT A JUNK SHOP. If they are playing anything other than the local AM radio station (and especially if they are playing CDs with pan pipes and bird calls), IT IS NOT A JUNK SHOP.

Alternatively, there's a good chance you've stumbled across a G.J.S. (Genuine Junk Shop) if any of the following are true:
- The shop, the stock and very likely the proprietor smell (musty, or worse).
- At least 30 per cent of the total weight of stock is made up by dust.
- Virtually none of the stock has a price ticket, but...
- The keener your initial price enquiry appears, the higher the price will be.
- You have no idea what at least half the stuff is and even less

idea why anyone would think that anyone else might buy it.
- There is a shelf of absolute must-have stuff next to which is a sign reading NOT FOR SALE.
- The proprietor calls every item in the shop by name.
- A dog is asleep somewhere where you have to step over it.
- Terms strictly cash and do not ask for credit as refusal often offends.

Trader Bob's in Goulburn was one of my finest J.S.D.s (Junk Shop Discoveries) ever. I walked through the door and immediately knew what I'd be doing for the next three hours. Yard, warehouse, shed, shop: the Quadrella. Just happened to stumble across it while on tour. The place was an absolute sub-zero bombsite of remnants, job lots and cast-offs. Favourites included the aircraft altimeter (marked 'works OK'), the leather pouches stamped '.303 INCH VICKERS LTD 1944', hundreds of assorted wooden shoe blocks, enamel post office signs, countless grease-encrusted mystery machinery parts and hundreds of hubcaps, none matching.

But the best bit was the artificial limbs. Four or five legs, hanging from the roof of the shop. Bob was rambling past when I asked him, 'How much for the artificial legs?' Bob stopped, turned, looked up, looked at me, counted my legs and without a hint of irony said, 'All depends how much you need 'em.' And on he shuffled to attend to his treasures.

I have two legs, so Bob wasn't about to get excited about

a sale. But if I'd been hopping on the spot, he'd have had the prosthetics down quicker than you can say Long John Silver.

He may not have clinched a sale, but Bob's philosophy has stayed with me. The more you need something, the harder you look. Amidst a tangle of trash, a jumble of junk, a labyrinth of litter lies treasure. It's the lure of the junk shop. Just imagine the thrill for the one-legged shopper in Goulburn. Tries every shop in town. Hops into Trader Bob's. Browses for hours. Then suddenly you hear the cries: 'Rejoice with me! I have found a new leg!'

In the same way, I tell you, there is rejoicing in the presence of the angels of God over one sinner who repents. Salvation. Now there's a treasure worth forsaking everything to find.

Attitude Makes the Difference

Philip Baker

I recently heard of a young man suffering with Down's Syndrome who worked at a checkout in a major supermarket. His job was to pack the bags of the customers as they came through his particular line.

He had, however, grabbed hold of the truth of attitude. He decided he would leave a signature on his work. He would do what he did better than everyone else around him.

He began to spend his evenings looking for quotes from books and the Internet, and when he had found a suitable one, he would write it up, photocopy it, then cut each page up so he had hundreds of little slips of paper with the quote of the day written on them. Then for the whole of the next working day he would put his 'Thought for the Day' into each bag he packed.

A couple of weeks went by and one day the store manager noticed that one checkout line had three times as many people as all the others. She quickly tried to organise more checkout operators and began to direct customers to these new open lines. To her surprise, she met great resistance. 'No,' people protested, 'we want to get our thought for the day.'

It didn't take long for that young man to become the store's most valuable employee. Whatever we do, attitude will make the difference.

The Little Things

Warwick Saxby

People involved in 'Christian ministry' tend to measure the success of their work by the degree to which they have affected the lives of others. I prefer to use a similar but different measure: to what degree have the lives of those I have sought to serve affected me?

We had been living in the Nimbin valley for some months. Our plan was to become as much a part of the community as we could. My wife Dianne had found a job in one of the many cafés in the village while I had begun my career as a bone carver and teller of stories that in one way or another pointed to Jesus. Our children attended Nimbin Central School. Each day we would compare notes, telling each other of the new, weird and wonderful things we had seen and experienced. There was plenty to learn in this, the capital of alternative Australia.

The house we first rented was very small, so when the opportunity came to move into a four-bedroom place we jumped at it. One day, without giving it a thought, the Christian lady who moved into our old house dropped off some of our mail at the café where Dianne worked. The top letter was addressed to 'Pastor Warwick Saxby'. Being a Christian in Nimbin is probably the easiest way to be universally unpopular. Being a representative of organised religion is almost the worst thing you could do in the eyes of many locals. Needless to say, when Jane at the café gave our letters to Dianne next time she arrived for work, the reception was cold indeed.

It was around this time that the people who were taking the vegetable scraps from the café to make compost for their organic farm decided to go into another line of work. With no one to take them, the overabundance of scraps at the café soon became a real problem. Dianne, feeling sympathy for her struggling employer, volunteered me to remove them. She told me a glowing story of the beautiful vegetables we could grow with all this fresh compost. There was one small problem: I had yet to construct the large compost bins necessary to handle the three or more huge garbage bins of veggie scraps produced by the café each day.

The days and weeks went by. Every afternoon I would drop off three clean, empty bins and take away three full ones. Every day that Jane was working I would greet her with a smile and a cheery hello, despite the fact that she usually ignored me and offered only the barest communication to Dianne when they worked together. Mind you, many of the other folk I met as I moved my cargo of scraps to our station wagon congratulated me on doing my part to help the environment.

Nearly five months passed with no sign of our relationship with Jane defrosting. Then one afternoon she stopped me and said that it had been good since I had been doing the compost scraps because I always brought the bins back clean. I was completely taken aback—not only had Jane spoken to me, she had chosen to compliment me! I could only think of one thing to say: 'What else would I do? It's a food shop; of course I'd bring them back clean.' She then told me that the previous people used to wash the bins at the back of the shop, which made the place stink. We parted with an awkward kind of friendliness.

Life went on more or less as normal for two more weeks. Then one day Dianne, eager to get home after a long day at work, was waiting in the car. I was on my way out of the café, having dropped off the last of the clean bins, when Jane stopped me to talk. She told me about life in Nimbin. She told me about her own personal struggles, her relationship with her husband, the fears they had for their son and the devastation wrought upon her daughter when she was sexually abused by a local businessman. Jane told me, a relative stranger whom until recently she could barely bring herself to acknowledge, things you would only tell the closest of confidants.

That was three years ago, and to this day, whenever I think about it, tears come to my eyes. I have never felt so humbled. Why did Jane tell me all these things? It certainly wasn't my title or any outward appearance. Five months of clean bins, that's why. Five months of consistently treating other people with respect. Five months of having integrity in the small things, things that matter to someone else.

It is easy to think that the little things don't matter, that nobody sees. But people do see. We are indeed surrounded by a cloud of witnesses, waiting to see Jesus living through us. And when they do see him, they are drawn to him—just as they always will be.

Miracle in Capernaum

Geoff Bullock

Dust and leaves started to fall from the roof—a little at first and then in great chunks. They fell on Jesus' head and the heads of those nearest him. Naturally everyone looked up, even the Pharisees.

Someone was on the roof. They were removing the tiles.

Faces appeared, and before much could be said, the hole was made so large that the sun streamed in. So much for the roof! Then, just when everyone thought they had seen everything, a man on a bed was lowered through the roof by four other men. He hovered in mid-air until he came to rest in front of Jesus.

The man was crippled.

All eyes turned from the roof to the man on the bed, to the dumbstruck Pharisees and finally to Jesus. What now?

It didn't take long. It happened so quickly, but it changed everything.

When He saw their faith, He said to him, 'Man, your sins are forgiven you.' And the scribes and the Pharisees began to reason, saying, 'Who is this who speaks blasphemies? Who can forgive sins but God alone?'

Good question.

But when Jesus perceived their thoughts, He answered and said to them, 'Why are you reasoning in your hearts? Which is easier, to say, "Your sins are forgiven you," or to say, "Rise up and walk"? But that you may know that the Son of Man has power on earth to forgive sins'—He said to the man who was paralysed, 'I say to you, arise, take up your bed, and go to your house.'

The man stood up, took his bedding and went home. And he was not quiet about it. As he walked out you could hear his friends sliding off the roof, shouting their heads off.

The Scribes and Pharisees where not impressed. They didn't even notice the healing. They noticed the blasphemy. Everyone did.

The man and his sickness may have been forgotten in the midst of the controversy. Controversy often disconnects our hearts as we try to use our heads. But Jesus had entered this man's story. His healing was not simply about the paralysis of his body. It went far deeper than that.

Look again and see what we so often miss. The poor man

was paralysed. His whole life was at the mercy of others. The climate of faith at that time presented him with the horrid distortion that his sickness resulted from God's judgment. Consequently he was paralysed in soul and spirit as well as body. Every day he lay under the judgment of God. His body was simply the evidence of God's displeasure.

Imagine what he felt when he heard that this Jesus of Nazareth may be the Messiah. Was he excited that God had come to his hometown of Capernaum? Or was he stricken with the fear that God had come to judge his sins personally? His friends came and told him the most wonderful things about this Jesus, but his heart could not receive it. Why? Because his God had sentenced him to this stretcher. His God was angry and demanded more of him than he could give. He had tried everything and everything was not enough. Obviously God knew something that he didn't, and it was this 'secret sin' that had sentenced his life to such horrid rejection. He feared this God.

It was easy to get excited when you hadn't fallen into God's hands. His friends were lucky—'blessed' with the favour of good health. He was not blessed. He was cursed. If the Messiah had turned up, then his worst fear had arrived.

His friends grabbed his stretcher. There was nothing he could do to stop them. They carried him into town, past the condescending stares of the marketplace, past the synagogue, through the milling crowds to Simon Peter's house. What were they doing?

Suddenly he was hoisted above the heads of the crowd, and before he knew it he was on the roof. He was absolutely humiliated—and worse was yet to come. His friends hatched a plan. They made a large hole by removing the tiles. He was going to be lowered through this hole, alone, to arrive guilty, judged and paralysed at the feet of Jesus. He was beyond himself with fear and he was powerless to stop them.

He was at their mercy, and soon he would be at the mercy of the Messiah.

Why were his friends doing this?

Perhaps it was simply because they wanted him to find out what he needed to do about the secret sin that must have caused God's judgment to fall on his stricken body. Perhaps Jesus would be able to tell their sick friend why this had happened, and what he should do so that God would lift the sentence of judgment.

But the poor man was in misery. His dark secret sins were about to be told to a house full of religious zealots, sins that were so great they had brought this horrible judgment on him. What on earth would God require from him to atone for whatever it was he had done? What sacrifice could he possibly afford? How would he present it?

It took an eternity to travel through the air above the heads of the crowd.

His eyes were clenched shut. He heard laughter and some poor jokes at his expense. He hit the floor with a jolt.

Silence.

He opened his eyes and looked into the face of God.

Jesus looked through this poor wretch's sickness and saw a heart that had been riddled with blasphemous lies. Jesus' first words to the cripple were the last ones the man thought he would ever hear. His guilt plagued his every thought. His guilt silenced all hope.

Jesus said, 'Man, your sins are forgiven you.'

Can you think of anything more wonderful? God came and stepped out of the fearful expectations of this poor paralytic and redefined himself in his paralysed spirit. What had barred his heart from ever hoping was now overwhelmingly overcome.

God came to forgive what this man could never forgive in himself. Why? Because his body lied to him. His spiritual community lied to him. He wouldn't have been able to accept forgiveness unless it came in the place of impending judgment. Just as depression sentences all its victims to a life devoid of happiness and hope, often without obvious cause, so too this man's guilt sentenced him to never being forgiven. He was guilty for no other reason than he was told that he should be, he must be, and his sickness proved it.

He lay at the feet of God, helpless, waiting for eternal wrath. He received eternal life, and the God of his expectations died as surely as the God of Jesus was resurrected in this cruel god's place.

He looked into the eyes of God expecting death and saw life.

Bible quotations are from Luke 5, NKJV.

A Tale of Two Pubs

Michael Frost

Recently it was reported that a congregation in a small rural town in Victoria had taken an innovative step toward reaching its community. A Melbourne newspaper announced, 'Patrons of the Hamilton Hotel will soon be offered spirit of a different kind. In an unusual conversion, the town's Baptist congregation—who are teetotallers—have taken over one of the six pubs.'

The Hamilton community watched in amazement as the pub, located in the main street opposite the local post office, was bought by the Baptists and renovated into a church and conference centre. Its front bar was turned into a recreation area for young people and its dance area was rebuilt into a chapel and meeting room. The bar was transformed into a coffee bar, the old pub now becoming an alcohol-free building.

In the article, various church leaders from Melbourne and the pastor of the Hamilton Baptist Church spoke of the relocation as innovative, creative and daring. However, one sour note was sounded. Midway through the newspaper article, a local from Hamilton was quoted: 'One of the hotel's former regulars, farmer Bruce McKellar, 71, said he would miss his corner of the bar. "I would walk in and straight to it; we all had our own space," he said.'

The implied sadness of this comment wasn't lost on me. Farmer McKellar had been displaced from his personal seat at the bar, and though he had probably moved on to one of the other pubs, he would never again be welcomed at his favourite watering hole. In Hamilton, farmers, tradesmen and business people had been shooed out of the Hamilton Hotel to make way for the Baptists.

Now this got me thinking. This project, though appearing innovative, is in fact Christendom-style thinking. It assumes that the church belongs prominently in the main street and it claims that the church has the right to take over a public space and clean out the local people while creating a so-called 'sanctified' religious zone. Whether it's in a pub, a school auditorium or a two-hundred-year-old cathedral, it represents the same thinking.

On the other side of the planet, in the English town of Bradford, another pub has been transformed by Christians. The Cock & Bottle is a yellow two-storey English pub at the bottom of the street on the corner of Bradford's inner ring road. Two years ago it was rented by the Bradford Christian

Pub Consortium. Bradford is a hardscrabble, working-class town. It has been noted in recent times for its racial conflict and street violence. But the Cock & Bottle represents a place of sanctuary and solace.

Malcolm Willis has been employed by the consortium to manage the pub, and he and his wife live upstairs above the bar. He proves himself to be a genuinely missional leader when he says, 'Jesus said, "Go into all the world." And this includes pubs. He didn't say sit in your church and wait for people to come to you.'

The Willises and their staff (all Christians) have set about creating a loving, welcoming environment where locals are cared for, listened to and ministered to. Says Willis, 'Initially, many won't accept you talking about Jesus. Maybe after you've listened to them ten or twenty times—which can be exhausting—they might say, "Can you pray for me?" And then you see things happen.' The missional church always thinks of the long haul rather than the quick fix.

Of course, the dilemma about whether Christians should be serving alcohol or not is bound to arise. Willis is himself a teetotaller, but he has an earthy and realistic outlook on the issue of drinking. 'Yes, we're selling booze to people who could do without it, but if we don't, they'll just go somewhere else. At least if they're here, we can get alongside them. I knew that when I came here I personally had to be seen not to drink, but I'm not everybody.

'Someone once showed me Proverbs 31, which says, "Beer and wine are only for the dying or for those who have lost all hope. Let them drink and forget how poor and miserable they feel. But you must defend those who are helpless and have no hope." So I have to ask: what would Jesus have done? I think the Lord would have been here in the pubs.'

I'm Rich!

Grenville Kent

Receiving a $500,000 cheque for our wedding was, well, quite helpful (even in Australian dollars). I pulled the cheque from the card and showed it to Carla, then darted away while she gasped, 'How many zeroes?'

'Half a million jumbuckeroonies,' I said.

'Let me see!'

Eventually she caught me and tackled me to the floor. 'Have a look,' I said.

She counted the zeroes. Five of them before the decimal point; two after.

'Who are Bernard and Collette?'

'Friends of mine,' I replied airily. 'Gold Coast business people.'

'I don't even know them!'

'Fantastic people.'

'I like them already.'

We visited my wife's parents to show them. My mother-in-law (MIL) trilled like a budgie on speed, not bothering to breathe for five minutes. My father-in-law (FIL) sat quietly, discombobulated.

'Who's this Bernard?' he said finally. 'Does he have this kind of money?'

'He's in Gold Coast real estate. Does very well.'

'Wow, you have some amazing friends.' They stared at the cheque for minutes, in case someone moved the numbers.

The party continued until my conscience couldn't stand it.

'Actually,' I said, 'it's a joke.'

'No!' boomed MIL, in denial. 'If he's rich and he's your friend, why?'

'Because Bernard loves a joke. And he already gave us a present—a book of inspirational quotations.'

'Oh,' she said, like a balloon deflating after the party.

'Sorry to kid you,' I said, 'but you were fun to watch.'

'At least we were rich for ten minutes,' said Carla, and we all had the good laugh Bernard wanted to give us.

We never took that cheque to the bank to cash in—and sometimes we treat God's promises like that. But God is different from Bernard in at least two ways. One, he's richer. And two, God isn't kidding. He makes huge promises and means them. Like: 'All who seek God will find joy in Him.'

'If we confess our sins, God will . . . forgive us and wash us clean . . .'

'Nothing can separate us from the love of God.'

'The peace of God that goes beyond logic will guard your heart and mind . . .'

'God will supply all your needs.'

Jesus promised, 'I will come again.'

'Whoever believes in me, even if they die, will live again.'

There are conditions to each promise, but they're carefully spelt out and they make sense.

Even God's commandments work like promises. When he says, 'You shall not steal', he's also saying, 'I promise you won't steal because my principles will make you successful and generous and honest, and I'll teach you how to be content.' When he commands us 'Love your enemies', that's a promise to help us see that even so-called jerks have hearts like our own with hurts and needs.

Bernard's cheque is taped onto the finance drawer of our filing cabinet. Every time we see it, we remind ourselves to claim all God's promises. 'He has given us incredibly large and valuable promises' with 'everything we need for life', and even the chance to 'share in God's own nature.'

Bible quotations are paraphrases drawn from Psalm 22:26; 1 John 1:9; Romans 8:35–39; Philippians 4:7, 19; John 14:3; John 11:25–26; 2 Peter 1:3–4.

The Power of Praise

Darlene Zschech

In May 2000, we were just about to go on a three-week Hillsong worship tour of the USA. These tours are very intense spiritually and physically, but the miracles we see happen through them are incredible.

I was twelve weeks pregnant at the time, with a child we had planned for and waited on for a very long time. One morning, three days before we were due to leave, my husband Mark and I went to the obstetrician to check the baby before we went on the tour—and found out that the child had just died in my womb.

Shattered, broken-hearted—all the words you can think of do not even come close to describing the agony of that moment. It was awful. Such a terrible loss. As any woman knows who has gone through this, your hopes and dreams for that child die as well.

We had taken separate cars to the doctor, so I had to drive back to the house by myself with Mark following me. I got in the car, and I just didn't know what to think or do. I can't describe the depth of sadness I was feeling.

On the way home, I heard the Holy Spirit whisper, 'Sing.'

In that moment, it was absolutely the last thing I wanted to do. Sing! Are you joking? But again I heard the Holy Spirit say, 'Sing.' After years of learning it is much better to obey quickly, I started to sing.

My head didn't sing and I don't even know if my heart sang, but my soul sang. It was almost involuntary. I sang two songs.

The first song that I heard coming out of my mouth was the hymn with the line: 'Then sings my soul, my Saviour God, to thee. How great thou art.' This really surprised me as this was a song that we sang at my father's funeral. The lyrics are about putting the Word of God above anything we could be humanly facing. Being triumphant in Him. The second song was one I had written years before called 'I Will Bless You, Lord'. The chorus says, 'How my soul cries out to you, O God. I will bless you, Lord.' Again, it wasn't my head singing. The core of my being, my soul, was singing rather than my intellect.

By the time I got home, something had definitely transpired in the spiritual realm. I had spoken many times on the power of worshipping through a trial. I had done this myself many times to varying degrees, but never before had I experienced the power of God so sovereignly coming and fulfilling his Word where it says, 'He heals the brokenhearted and binds up their wounds' (Psalm 147:3). Through being in the sweet presence of our glorious Saviour, I was well on the way to complete healing and personal victory.

I still had to go through the physical ramifications of losing a child—the operation, telling our girls, telling our church (who were so excited for us). And hours and hours of tears.

But Mark and I made the decision to continue with our plans and go on the worship tour. It was probably one of the hardest things I have ever done. But again, night after night, I found myself saturated in God's presence as I led worship from a position of faith. I chose to lead worship and not give the enemy any more ground than he had already taken. For three weeks, I continually made a daily decision to lift my eyes and praise God with all I had.

I found my healing in the arms of God. Even though grief still took its natural course, I found the truth of 'Sing, O barren woman . . .' And I thank God for, and will always treasure, the child that I got to mother for twelve weeks.

Giving out of Poverty

Amanda Smith

When Jesus looked up and saw the poor widow giving two small coins, he was touched by her willingness to give all she had. Her two coins were nothing, but to her they were everything. We know this story well and we apply it to our financial giving. We understand that Jesus is concerned not about dollar amounts but about our heart and about the percentage of our income that we are willing to give.

But does this story have more to teach us?

Rachel is a dedicated Christian. She fasts regularly and spends an hour reading her Bible, journalling and praying every day. Her conversation is filled with references to her Lord and how he touches her life. She is rich in her spiritual walk.

And yet she is in abject poverty in other areas of her life. As the child of an addict, she struggles with addictive behaviour herself. She recently called, discouraged, after a weekend of overindulgence. 'If I give in to my addictions, does it mean God doesn't have my heart?' she cried.

Suddenly the story of the poor widow came to mind.

Rachel is able to give generously to God out of her wealth, but it is impossible for her to give the same amount out of her poverty. For a TV addict to go a whole weekend without TV is for her to give all she has. For a child of abuse to go one day without screaming at his own children is for him to give all he has. For a recovering gossip to hold her tongue once is to give all she has.

God doesn't compare how much we give to how much others give. He compares how much we give to how much we have.

Rachel now carries two pennies in her pocket every day. They serve to remind her that although she is poor, she is giving all she has to God.

More Beyond

Gordon Moyes

I was visiting a member of my church who was in the cancer ward of a public hospital. As I finished speaking and praying with him, the charge nurse came and asked if I would mind visiting an Italian man who was close to death and wanted to see a priest.

I introduced myself and explained I wasn't a Roman Catholic priest but would be pleased to pray with him and read some Scripture. In halting English he gripped my hand and told me he knew me from watching my television program on Sundays. That seemed to make my presence with him even more significant than that of a priest.

I asked his name. It was Colombo. 'Like the fictional TV detective?' I asked. He protested, saying he was born in Genoa, and then adding a great deal I didn't understand. He painfully repeated it and I got it at last—he was named after that city's most famous son, Christopher Columbus.

He knew that he would live only a matter of hours or a

day or so, and was fearful of death. I told him of the great promises Jesus gave us of life after death, and how, through faith, we could pass through death into the life beyond.

As I shared with him my belief in life after death, he said, in broken English, 'I wish I could believe it. If only I could believe that there is life on the other side, I would have no fear now.'

I told him that this life is not the end, that there is more beyond, that death is a door that opens up to new life, and that Jesus has removed our fear of death. And then suddenly I had an inspiration.

'Do you remember that in the days of Christopher Columbus people thought the world was flat?' I asked. 'If a sailor went too far he would come to the edge and drop off.'

He remembered.

'In those days,' I continued, 'people believed the heavens were held up by two great pillars at the entry to the Mediterranean Sea, called the Pillars of Hercules. You could sail through them, but they had to be kept in sight in order to be safe.'

Colombo nodded. He knew.

'In the reign of Philip and Isabella,' I went on, 'Spain had coins that pictured the Pillars of Hercules and the words in Latin *Ne plus ultra*—no more beyond. Then, in 1492, your Christopher Columbus sailed across the ocean and found land and people on the other side. From the West Indies he brought back people of a different colour. He gave the monarchs wonderful gifts. He said, "There is land beyond. There is more beyond." Spain took its coins and crossed off the word *Ne* and left the words *plus ultra*.'

Colombo nodded again. He understood, and smiled at me with absolute joy.

'There is more beyond!' I told him. 'When Jesus Christ came back from the dead, he said, "There is more beyond. You need not fear. I am going there to prepare a place for you. And if I go and prepare a place for you, I will come back and take you to be with me that you also may be where I am." We need not fear that death is the end. There is more beyond.'

He gripped my hand with all of his strength, his eyes full of tears but his heart at peace. A few days later I returned, but Colombo had died.

Several weeks later a large parcel arrived. It was from a member of Colombo's family. Colombo had told him to send me one of his possessions when he died and to get a brass plate made.

It was a very old and beautifully constructed model ship about 40 centimetres long in full rigging. On the mainsail was a cross. It was a model of the Santa Maria, the ship in which Christopher Columbus sailed. On the stand was a small brass plate with the words, 'More Beyond'.

Today it stands in my study reminding me of what I have just told you, and encouraging me to look to the life beyond.

Aced by Despair

Margaret Court and Barbara Oldfield

Margaret Court is Australia's greatest tennis champion, but after her retirement in 1976 she was dogged by feelings of fear, insecurity and inferiority. These feelings were compounded by a form of Christian teaching that emphasised radical introspection about past hurts and insecurities. In 1979 Margaret was hospitalised ...

'I became totally self-centred with all this emphasis on looking in at myself,' Margaret says. 'I was not really aware of my family either, almost to the point of neglect, as I consistently analysed my life to see why I felt so guilty, unworthy, fearful and totally insignificant. My self-esteem crumbled under this type of scrutiny. I truly did not even feel human any more. I wept and cried all the time in a state of emotional distress. I had nothing to anchor my hope on and floated about in a sea of bewilderment until I was nothing more than a shipwrecked shell.'

Even the normal pride she felt in having been the world's

best tennis player was now seen to be a bad thing that she needed to deal with. It was labelled an 'evil spirit' that needed to be cast out of her. This only magnified her fear, for now she had things to deal with she had never considered before. She began to think that she needed to be set free from anything that could even remotely be considered an ungodly part of her life. Over time Margaret began to feel she was in the grip of Satan himself.

Confusion, disappointment and self-hatred took a mighty hold on her life. Fear opened the door to physical illness. Her once powerful, muscular frame became emaciated. Her lack of peace, confused thoughts and resulting emotional instability all took a terrible toll.

There was such torment in Margaret's life that to this day she remembers its awesome power. At times she felt it was like a type of paralysis, leaving her unable to perform the simple, mundane functions of her own household. Her mind was like a windmill turning over and over, with dreadful thoughts flooding her head incessantly. Sleep was only possible with the help of sleeping tablets; her mind just could not stop ticking over. Insomnia became a way of life, and soon severe depression descended over her like a large, black storm cloud.

'When morning came I wished it was night and when night came I wished it was morning,' she relates. 'I had no peace, either awake or fitfully asleep; it didn't matter. I really thought that if it was going to be like this on earth then I would rather go home and be with God. I was of no use to anybody; not to myself, my family or even to God.'

Hearing all the arguments, however logical and rational, as to why such terror was unwarranted did not ease her situation at all. Being told that she had so much to live for, with a devoted husband and family and enough wealth accumulated for the remainder of her life, only produced further guilt, because she knew there was no reason for her to feel the way she felt—but she did!

The discovery of 2 Timothy 1:7 turned her whole life around forever.

For God has not given us a spirit of fear, but of power and of love and of a sound mind. (NKJV)

At first this was the only scripture she could memorise entirely because her mind was still very confused. Over and over she said it; day and night, night and day. She personalised it: 'God has not given *me* the spirit of fear, but of power, and of love, and of a sound mind.' She constantly repeated it when fear, doubt and confusion tried to take back the small amount of ground they had lost to this positive affirmation. It was beginning to push them from their stronghold over her mind. The more she spoke it, the more her mind began to believe what she said—and slowly it began to act as if it was so.

Somehow—she did not really know how—the fear started

to diminish. Her mind stopped spinning in circles. Now she was able to read and memorise further scriptures. She began to take the Bible as her 'spiritual medicine', just as she was still taking her physical medication. She learnt that as she was speaking scriptural statements over herself daily, she was washing herself in the water of God's Word. Slowly she sensed many other areas of her life also changing, and it was all good.

Her diligence during her tennis years to train and apply herself to the arduous task of getting her body into peak physical condition now paid off. She applied the same diligence to keeping the Word of God before her eyes and in her mouth at all times—especially the scriptures that were relevant to her particular problems. Now she felt she understood clearly why she had suffered so much: she had never read, meditated on and attended to the Word. She was determined that it would never escape her attention again. It held the key to her salvation, healing, wholeness, soundness and general well-being. It was the solid basis on which she had to build her faith.

Meeting the Megastar

John Dickson

If you'd asked me at sixteen whom I'd like to meet more than anyone else in the world, I would have said, 'Bono from U2', for sure. But how on earth do you meet the lead singer of one of the biggest rock bands in the world? These guys apparently earn $200 a minute, each. Why on earth would they bother with a starry-eyed teenager just starting out in his first band?

When they toured Australia I tried ringing the five-star hotel where they were staying and saying that I was the 'brother' of the Edge (U2's guitarist). I had heard they were Christians so I figured I wasn't *exactly* lying. The lady at the desk politely hung up on me.

Then one of my friends had an idea. She suggested I dress up, go to the hotel and hang around in the lobby as if I were a hotel guest. So that's what I did. The next day, a friend and I dressed up in suits and ties, got ourselves briefcases and caught a taxi straight to the hotel door. To our surprise the doorman opened the door and showed us straight into the hotel, right past the U2 fans who were banned from entering. We hung around in one of the hotel shops until, sure enough, the Edge and Larry Mullen Jr (U2's drummer) walked out of the lift toward us. We pounced on them and spent the next five or ten minutes getting things signed, taking photos and asking countless questions.

We were wrapped—so wrapped we went straight home, told our mates and made plans for another attempt.

The next day, about eight of us dressed up in suits, got briefcases and caught taxis in convoy to the hotel. The same thing happened. The doorman opened the door and showed us straight past a bunch of very suspicious U2 fans, right into the hotel. This time we headed for the restaurant. There we ordered toast and bottomless coffee. We must have hung around in that place for three hours, waiting for the band to arrive for breakfast. At about 11.30 a.m. Bono came in and sat at a table right near us. I left him alone with his breakfast partner for about ten minutes and then introduced myself and asked if he had the time to meet my mates. He said he'd love to, just as soon as he finished recording the interview he was in the middle of. I look down and there on the table was a tape recorder, still recording. Oops! About fifteen minutes later he came over to our table and chatted and signed all the stuff we had managed to cram into our briefcases.

About ten minutes later, as I finished my fifth or so coffee for the morning, the hotel manager walked over to our table. We braced ourselves and got ready to be thrown out. He looked at us. 'Lads,' he said, 'I know exactly what you've been doing all morning. I like your initiative. Stay as long as you like.' We couldn't believe our ears! We were so happy we bought another round of toast and coffee.

When we finally left, all the other U2 fans outside the hotel yelled abuse at us and made all sorts of interesting finger signs. But I didn't mind—I had met the guys from U2.

People have always done ridiculous things to get the attention of famous people, things you'd never dream of doing to meet a 'normal' person. With Jesus it was no different. It's easy to forget that in his time Jesus was as popular as an individual could get. No one else drew the crowds he drew. On one occasion, well over 5000 men (not even counting women and children) gathered to hear him. Admittedly, Gillian Anderson (from *The X-Files*) drew a crowd of 10,000 at a recent in-store appearance, but her fans only had to go to their local shopping centre. Jesus' admirers often had to travel out into the countryside, on foot, just to get to hear him.

Everyone wanted to meet him: politicians, children, peasants, soldiers, priests, criminals, kings, everyone. He soon became the unrivalled Megastar of his time, and for good reason, I think. People longed to hear him say to them: 'Friend, your sins are forgiven.'

September Agent

Irene Voysey

International award-winning photographer Ken Duncan is well known in Australia for his panoramic photography and his outspoken Christian beliefs. But four years ago, even Christians doubted Duncan's sanity when he began to say he believed that God wanted him to give the American nation a message through his work.

Enduring the scepticism of others was not a problem for Ken Duncan. He had already endured countless hardships on his many journeys into wilderness areas as he sought the quintessential photograph. Now, to fulfil what he saw as an assignment from God, he was prepared to face any new challenges. The first, and what seemed to be the biggest one, came in early 1998. Unlike others he had faced, this one wasn't in the wilderness, but in New York.

Ken had gone to a meeting with one of America's largest publishers and was pleased when they immediately expressed enthusiasm for his proposal that they publish a book of his

Panographs®, covering all fifty American states. But the enthusiasm waned when he said he already had a title for the book. It was to be called *America Wide: In God We Trust*.

The publisher's problem was not with *America Wide* but with the phrase *In God We Trust*. 'It will be too politically sensitive,' they said. Ken's reminder that the phrase appeared on every American dollar note fell on deaf ears. The publishers were regretful but insistent that such a title would not help sell the book. A second leading publisher was even more adamant that if the book was to sell well in America there should be no reference to God at all, either on the cover or in any of the text.

Ken returned to Australia, down but still determined. After breaking the news to his wife, Pam, that the American publishers would not accept his terms, he said earnestly, 'Pam, we must publish this book ourselves. It's a huge project and will cost us everything we own and more. Are you with me in this?' Pam did not hesitate. 'What we own isn't ours anyway,' she said, 'it all belongs to God.'

Over the next three years Ken flew from Australia to America thirty-four times, eventually photographing all fifty American states. It was exhausting and expensive work, but even as he captured America's spectacular scenery, Ken believed God was guiding him and giving him unique opportunities for his own purposes. Further encouragement came in the form of sponsors such as American Airlines, the Bank of America, Qantas and Fujifilm. 'Each time I needed support during that whole period, it came just in time,' he says.

At the book's launch in Sydney, Ken referred to the opening words of the Introduction. They are taken from a speech made in a church by Abraham Lincoln in 1838. Lincoln asked, 'At what point shall we expect the approach of danger? By what means shall we fortify against it?' Like Lincoln, Duncan too spoke of the dangers from within the nation: of spiritual waywardness, such as the banning of prayer in state schools and the lack of teaching of the Ten Commandments. His concluding words at the launch were uncannily prophetic: 'There will be powers which will come against this great nation and I believe God wants to remind the American people to continue to put their trust in him because of who he is.'

America Wide: In God We Trust was launched just four days before September 11, 2001.

The Australian Prime Minister, John Howard, was preparing to depart for America at that time. Shortly before the launch of the book, he was shown a copy of *America Wide: In God We Trust*, and it was suggested he take the newly published book as a gift for US President George W. Bush. Mr Howard agreed and graciously asked if Ken would include a personal note to President Bush. Ken gladly accepted and wrote to the President, saying he believed God had led him to produce this book as a reminder to the

American people to put their trust in him.

The Prime Minister left for America on September 8. On September 10, he presented *America Wide: In God We Trust* to President Bush.

On September 11 terrorists launched an attack on America that brought down the twin towers of the World Trade Centre and focused the eyes of the world on a crippled and grief-stricken nation.

In the spiritual renewal that swept the United States in the wake of that disaster, *America Wide: In God We Trust* proved to be a book that brought comfort and new hope to many thousands of Americans. By May 2002 the book was into its fourth print-run in America.

Ken Duncan, who risked so much to be God's agent, continues to pray that obedient trust in God will become a reality for Americans tempted to live in fear of an enemy who lurks in the shadows.

Fair Dinkum with God

Kel Richards

(Luke 18:9–14)

> Two blokes wandered into a church
> In the midst of a country town.
> The day was hot, the church was cool,
> The sun was blazing down.
>
> The church was old and built of stone,
> It was cool in the summer heat.
> The doors stood open invitingly,
> Welcoming weary feet.
>
> David Gently was a cattleman
> And a Shire Council member,
> Wearing his new imported suit
> Even in a hot December.

Sam Hunt was a used car dealer,
He was known as 'Slippery Sam'.
He'd always put one over you
With a dodgy sort of scam.

Both sat down in the cool and the shade
And both began to think.
While Gently's pride was swelling,
Sam's heart began to shrink.

The thoughts in David Gently's head
Were all about his qualities,
About his upright 'niceness'
And lack of foolish frivolities.

But Slippery Sam began to feel
A creeping sort of shame.
He thought of the dodgy deals he'd done
And the people he'd caused some pain.

'Dear God,' thought David Gently,
'I'm glad I'm as nice as I am,
Religious and well-respected,
And not like Slippery Sam.'

A tear trickled down the cheek
Of wicked old Slippery Sam.
'Forgive me, God,' is what he thought,
'I'm not a nice sort of man.'

And as those two walked back outside
To the heat that boiled and fried,
Slippery Sam, in the eyes of God,
Was the one who was justified.

To those whom God finds humble
And fair dinkum, he'll give a place,
While who have their nose in the air
Are sure to fall flat on their face.

Come Home

Brian Pickering

In July 1999 some 400 prayer leaders and intercessors representing the Anglo and Aboriginal churches in Australia gathered at Uluru. We came to be reconciled, to honour each other before God, and to pray for the healing of our nation.

During our time together, one of the leaders expressed a concern for those who had been hurt by fellow Christians and had left the church, as well as for pastors who had given up their calling in brokenness, often hurt by critical parishioners. Others expressed concern for those who had backslidden in their faith and for those who had not yet even met up with Jesus. We began to cry out to God for all of these folk. After several minutes the prayers began to form into a call of 'Come Home, Come Home', which went out across the vast open spaces around us for maybe five or ten minutes. This call was to those for whom we were praying, urging them to 'Come Home' to the Father who loved them and understood everything they had experienced, the Father who offered healing and reconciliation with himself and with Christian brothers and sisters.

The whole time of prayer around the 'Come Home' call lasted no more than a quarter of an hour, and after it finished we went on with other prayers. Nothing more was thought of what we had done until we got home and began to receive e-mails, phone calls and letters from all over the nation telling of strange encounters that people were having with Jesus.

The following Sunday a young lady in her early twenties attended a church in country New South Wales for the first time. The pastor, knowing her to be a visitor, greeted her as she left the service and asked her why she was worshipping with them that morning. She explained that she was the daughter of missionaries working in Papua New Guinea, but that while attending university in Sydney she had lost her faith and had not attended a church for six years. The pastor enquired further: why on that Sunday had she returned to church after such an absence? During the week, she said, she had had a vivid dream in which she had seen Jesus standing at the foot of her bed, beckoning to her with his hand and speaking the words, 'Come home, come home. All is forgiven. Come home'. So vivid was the dream that she decided then and there to come back to church that Sunday. When asked which night she had the dream, she replied, 'Wednesday'—the day the 'Come Home' call had gone out from Uluru.

In a motel room in Darwin on the very same night, a former Aboriginal pastor who had backslidden from the church and his relationship with the Lord was awoken at 4.00 a.m. by the 'presence' of a figure dressed in white in his room. This presence was a man whom he recognised as Jesus. As he looked at the figure before him, he saw him beckoning to 'Come home, come home'. So real was this experience for him that the next morning he immediately went to the home of a pastor friend to tell of his encounter with Jesus a few hours before, and to recommit his life to the Lord and begin the process of returning to his first calling as a preacher. Another prodigal son had returned home in response to the prophetic prayer uttered at Uluru.

Several months later I was in Tasmania telling some of the stories of what had been happening in our nation in response to prayer. Among them I told several stories of how God had answered our prayer for the 'lost' to return home. I felt quickened to invite the people present to again cry out to God for those who had left home, either spiritually or physically. Again the 'Come Home' call rang out, this time into the heavens over Hobart. I also asked people to name those they wished to call home.

The next day a woman ran up to me. 'You wouldn't believe what happened to our family last night,' she said excitedly. 'I was at the meeting yesterday when we called home those who had left home and had become estranged, either from their family or from God. When I got home from the meeting last night my daughter, who left home some four or five years ago and who has refused to speak with her father in all that time, was sitting in our lounge room talking to him. After years of bitterness, they had been reconciled even before I got home. It's a miracle!'

There are many more stories to tell, and the 'Come Home' call still goes out from time to time in different places and circumstances as the Lord moves us by his Spirit. Whenever it is given, we always seem to hear of those who are impacted by it, not because of what we do, but because of God's heart to restore those who are hurt, wounded and lost to the household of God. He wants us all to 'Come Home' to the intimacy of relationship with him for which we were created.

God answers prayer, not only for the individual person who seeks him, but also for the 'unknown' thousands out there who cannot pray for themselves but rely on the prayers of others to change their circumstances.

Lesson in a Petrol Station

Kim Hawtrey

It happened on our annual family vacation one year.

We were driving back from Melbourne to Sydney after a delightful week spent seeing the sights of Victoria. The kids were asleep in the back seat and we were sharing the driving.

Nearing the state border with New South Wales we needed to stop for petrol. I pulled into the service station and drew up alongside the bowser. My wife, Jenny, said she would check the oil, while I agreed to look after the petrol.

Oil checked, Jenny said she needed to visit the bathroom. Meanwhile I was distracted by the kids who, now wide awake, were asking the usual questions: 'Where are we, Dad?' 'Are we there yet?' 'I'm cold—where's my jumper?' Minutes passed. At one stage, out of the corner of my eye, I noticed Jenny inside the convenience store section of the service station, talking with the station operator. She must be taking care of business, I thought.

Another few moments went by, and at last the kids were settled again. Jenny had returned to the car and was seated ready to leave. I took my place again behind the driver's wheel, fastened my seat belt and began to move the car out of the driveway. Checking for traffic, I pulled out onto the highway and we were off again, continuing our journey.

We were making good time, and ten or fifteen minutes must have passed as we cruised onward.

Casually I asked Jenny a question: 'How much oil did the car take?'

'A litre,' she replied.

'How much did they charge?' I asked.

'I have no idea,' she answered. 'Why don't you check the receipt—after all, you're the one who paid . . .'

I sat upright. 'I didn't pay for the petrol. I thought you did,' I said.

'No, I thought you did,' said Jenny, equally startled.

The reality was, neither of us had paid. We had left without settling our account.

Immediately, I turned the car around and headed back to the service station. The owner was pleased to see us. He had already called the police—it was routine procedure—and they were ready to stop us at the next town. We were like a kind of Bonnie and Clyde, fugitives on the run!

I apologised to the proprietor and paid the amount due. He took it in good humour once I explained what had happened. It had all been due to a simple misunderstanding. Just a breakdown in communication between my wife and me, that's all.

Communication. It's such an important word. Think about it for a moment.

How many wars could have been prevented down through history if only there had been better communication?

How many marriages might be saved today if there was simply stronger communication between the parties?

And most important of all, how many souls might yet be saved for eternity if only those same souls would communicate with their Maker—while there is still time.

Finding God in the Mud

Michael Frost

Australia's most famous twentieth century author, Patrick White, is the only Australian ever to win a Nobel Prize for literature. In his older years, White was living a reclusive life in a small farm just outside Sydney. It was the 1970s and White was domiciled with his gay partner, Manoly, but passing him off as his housekeeper/assistant. He had already won the Nobel, so he was famous and independent, living comfortably if secretively in so-called sexually repressed Australia.

In his autobiography, White relates that this was a period when he felt enormously powerful, full of his own worth. After all, he was internationally famous and a local hero. His books sold well and he felt like the master of his own destiny.

Then one day, after it had been raining almost continually for days, he put on his raincoat and galoshes, loaded up a tray full of bowls of dog food and ventured out into the rain to feed his many farm dogs. As he stepped into the sodden yard, both his feet slid out from under him and he landed heavily on his backside in the mud. In his account of the incident, White says that he was in so much pain he could barely move, and as he lay there coated in sloppy dog food and mud he looked up into the angry black sky as large raindrops fell on his face.

He says that at that moment he had an epiphany. He began to laugh heartily in spite of the pain. Here he was, the greatest writer of his generation, lying helplessly in this sludge as a force much greater than he rained down on him. His enduring feeling was one of someone or something saying to him, 'Who the hell do you think you are?'

Later, while being attended to by Manoly, White, still shaken by the accident, said to his partner, 'We must get ourselves to church.' This experience of encountering his puniness in the midst of the cosmos so affected him that he, although a vehement critic of the church, immediately thought he must reconnect with God.

In White's day, it was assumed that the only place to meet God was in church. Sadly, when he and Manoly went to the local Church of England service that Sunday, the rector trumpeted from the pulpit that he had seen members of his parish entering a jellybean guessing competition at the recent local town fair. This, he declared, was gambling and required the immediate repentance of those involved.

The God presented in church was a finicky one, easily

upset about minor details and tiny infractions of some prescribed code. The God whom White thought he had heard in the mud in his backyard was one of majesty and breathtaking power and grace. In his autobiography, White says that he and Manoly resolved that whatever faith they had would remain an entirely private matter.

Patrick White did not become a Christian as far as I know, though he certainly responded to God's gracious expression of love. Grace, I believe, is everywhere. The church should recognise this fact, and be more concerned than it is to live in close proximity with not-yet-Christians as they stumble over God's always-present grace, helping tease out their responses to this God who loves them.

The Strangest Gift

Phillip Jensen

It was when my grandmother's eyes twinkled with delight that I knew she had finally lost the plot completely.

I was only a small boy when I came to that judgment. It was Christmas Day, and I had just opened my grandmother's present to me in front of the rest of the family. Our tradition was to open the presents one at a time for everybody to see and share in the pleasure of giving and receiving.

When the time had come for her gift, I undertook the usual little boy activity of shaking the unopened package. I heard a rattle that gave the portent of pleasure but no great insight into its contents. On opening it I delivered the customary response taught to all polite young boys: 'Thank you, Nan, it's just what I wanted.'

Her face beamed, and it was then—at that precise moment—that I saw the twinkle in her eye which confirmed my judgment: she had lost the plot completely.

For some time I had suspected that my grandmother was not the full two shillings. Her cheating at cribbage generally relied on a failure to remember the rules—not that the rules of cribbage are hard to remember. Her hours in front of the newspaper completely asleep seemed to be developing into a permanent posture. Her inability to engage me in conversation about the important matters of life—like the exploits of cricketing legends Keith Miller and 'Typhoon' Tyson—was growing apace. She was the relative with the least grasp on the reality of life!

And then I saw the twinkle in her eye and knew she really had altogether lost the plot. The family were all laughing and I did not know how to help her further embarrassment. I figured that the obligatory grandson kiss on the cheek would not go astray. So I performed the required service with mixed emotions of pleasure (for she was a loving old woman) and pity, tinged with confusion, for I really did not know what to say or do.

What do you say or do when your grandmother has delivered to you as your Christmas present a small plastic container of her laxatives?

The place was in pandemonium. Christmas was full of hilarity at the best of times and, surrounded by presents, wrapping paper, food, drink and relatives on all sides, the jocularity seemed overwhelming.

'Open it,' she whispered to me.

With embarrassed hands I undid the top to look at the dreaded tablets rattling inside the packet. The profusion of threepenny pieces that tumbled out all over my little fingers created a strange range of emotions. Relief that it was not laxatives. Enjoyment at being tricked. Pleasure that she had given me so much money. Embarrassment that the family was laughing at me, not her.

And understanding of those twinkling eyes. She had outwitted me.

My well-mannered reception of her gift had masked an arrogant disdain for the giver. I did not appreciate the value of what I had been given. I did not respect or trust the person who gave it to me. I was too full of my own prejudicial pride to bother carefully examining the gift.

It is more blessed to give than to receive, but it takes more humility to receive than to give. How often people treat God's great gift of Jesus with my childish prejudicial pride, making the offensively polite responses while despising the giver.

Big Plan

Angela Eynaud

When I was little, my great-uncle Bob used to drop by occasionally for a visit. He would ruffle my dark curls and exclaim with utter conviction, 'This one's going to be Miss Australia.' He was so confident that I believed it would happen one day.

My mother also used to tell me that the half-moon-shaped birthmark on my inner wrist was a secret sign that I was a fairy princess in disguise. One day the fairies would claim me and I'd get my wings back. On warm days, when the mark stood out more obviously, I'd look at it and wonder. I so much wanted to believe that it, too, would happen.

Other fantasy stories about my future came from visiting ministers and from people on Christian youth camps. 'God has BIG plans for your future,' they would say. I heard testimonies along these lines: 'My teacher/father/mother told me I'd never amount to anything and for years, though I wanted to be a pop star/doctor/Olympic athlete, I believed I was no good. Then I found Jesus and I knew they were wrong. God has a plan for my life.' Often the message went on: 'Don't limit God by thinking small. Dream BIG dreams.' Unfortunately the dreams then offered as examples bore more resemblance to the Miss Australia/fairy princess scenarios than what I now understand to be God's plan for his children.

God's BIG plans almost invariably were visions of career success. Careers as world leaders, managing directors or sports stars were what God's children might expect. Of course, some speakers offered stardom in the church: a missionary who converts thousands of Muslims, a pastor of a large church or the next Amy Grant. Seldom did I hear anyone encourage me to aspire to be a good bank teller, a dedicated Sunday school teacher or the kindest neighbour in my street.

As I approach my fortieth birthday and engage in some mid-life naval gazing, it strikes me that it's too late. I've missed my chance. I never did become Miss Australia, the fairies never came and the BIG plans never eventuated. My life is full and rich and challenging, but it's clear I'm decidedly small-time. My artistic and musical talents are second-rate, and I probably won't write a novel to rival *Lord of the Rings* after all.

As I look at how God's plans turned out for those who sat beside me at the youth camps, I see that none of them made it big either. One of my Christian friends battles with the challenge of raising a son with severe learning and behavioural problems. Another is trying to balance mothering two small boys and working part-time as a GP. She expressed her frustration to me, saying, 'I'm neither a good mother nor a good doctor.' A couple have gone to a mission field where even one convert would be a rich return for years of effort.

If we measured the success of our lives by the definitions offered in our youth, we'd all be failures.

What God considers successful may not resemble our definition. God's plans may well look BIG only from his eternal perspective. Consider St Monica, who was canonised by the Roman Catholic Church for her faithfulness in praying for the conversion of her son, Augustine. As she travailed in prayer for her wayward son, she probably didn't consider herself a potential saint.

While I wait for greatness to be thrust upon me, I'll love and serve those God has put within my small circle—my family, students, friends, neighbours. That's enough of a challenge for a lifetime.

God does have a big dream for me. He will gradually turn me into someone who resembles his Son. That's better than being Miss Australia. Mind you, I haven't quite given up waiting for those fairies.

Rita and Evonne

Dave Andrews

Some of our most marginalised neighbours are people who have been deinstitutionalised. They have been put out of psychiatric hospitals in the hope that, by being placed in a community rather than in an institution, their lives will be normalised. However, most of the people being placed in our community are not placed with families. After all, very few families—even their own—would welcome them home. So they are being placed in hostels.

When our family started visiting the hostels, it became painfully obvious that the vast majority of the people living there had no significant reciprocal relationships with people living outside the hostels—other than with those, like case workers, who were paid to relate to them.

It was a state of affairs that we felt was not very healthy for anyone's sense of self-esteem. So Evonne, my daughter—then her sister Navi—decided they would try to befriend a few people in a local hostel.

Evonne decided she would try to get alongside a woman whom I shall refer to as Rita. Now Rita was pretty much completely friendless. And, to be frank, one of the major reasons she had no friends was that no one who knew her well really wanted to be her friend! Rita was very difficult to relate to. I must confess that I've occasionally described her, in jest, as 'the grumpiest woman in the world'; and no one I know who knew her—not even Evonne, who loved her dearly—ever said that my description was unfair!

I first met Rita when she came up behind me, unexpectedly, and pushed me off the chair I was sitting on. I looked up and there was a very angry, chubby seventy-year-old woman staring down at me, snarling, 'That's my chair, mister!'

I looked around and saw that the room had sixty or seventy empty chairs scattered round it. I suggested that surely she could have taken another seat if she wanted one, as the one I'd been sitting on was exactly the same as all the others. But she just said, 'That's my chair, mister! Get another one yourself.'

In my next encounter with her, Rita continued her policy of driving right over the top of me like a heavily-laden truck rolling over a speed bump. One night I remember serving tea and biscuits when I saw her approaching the counter at full speed. I gave her a cup of tea and was just in the middle of asking her to take only one biscuit till everyone had a chance to have one when she thrust both mitts into the biscuit tin, grabbed as many biscuits as her chubby fists could hold, and stuffed them all into her mouth at once!

I wasn't the only one who found Rita difficult to relate to. When I took people from her hostel out on picnics, I noticed that no one wanted to sit next to her on the bus. I think it had something to do with the fact that whenever some of the more frail and less mobile people were getting on or off the bus, Rita would scream at them, push them aside and barge her way through. So it was not uncommon for our outings to begin and end with the bizarre ritual of everyone on the bus chanting, 'We hate you, Rita! We hate you, Rita! We hate you, Rita!'

Now my daughter Evonne has always had a love for stray dogs, and indeed for underdogs of all kinds. Because everyone we knew avoided Rita like the plague—like she had rabies— Evonne went out of her way to get to know her.

Evonne began by dropping in to visit Rita at the hostel where she lived. To begin with, Rita was not taken with Evonne. But her eyes lit up when Evonne invited her out to the Café Babylon for coffee and cheesecake. Rita liked her biscuits but she *loved* her cheesecake. And I think it was by offering to treat her to cheesecake that Evonne won Rita's heart.

Each Tuesday morning, before going to art college, Evonne would drop into Rita's room at the hostel. Rita would be up, ready and waiting, dressed in her glad rags. When Evonne arrived they would help each other finish off the last touches to each other's makeup, and, in spring, maybe even put a flower in their hair. Then they would be off.

They made an odd couple: a happy twenty-year-old girl with a bounce in her step, walking down the street with a crabby seventy-year-old woman shuffling beside her, muttering every step of the way. But in time the locals got used to seeing this odd pair making their way to the café.

When they got there the order would always be the same—coffee and cheesecake. To begin with Rita could barely contain her excitement and, on occasions, was known to jump the gun and grab a slice of cheesecake sitting temptingly on a plate in front of another customer at a nearby table. Evonne would then have to restrain Rita while she was trying to calm an irate customer whose cheesecake had been eaten before their very eyes.

However, as time went by, Rita began to trust Evonne. If Evonne said Rita's cheesecake would come, it would come. Evonne would make sure of it. So Rita started to relax and learn to enjoy her coffee while waiting for her cheesecake.

As the weeks passed, bit-by-bit, Rita began to share her story with Evonne. When she was nineteen, Rita was deemed a troublesome person and was sent to a local psychiatric hospital. There she was confined for the next forty years. During that time she lost contact with all her family and friends. She felt as if she actually had no family, had no friends—that the only one she could count on to look after her was herself. So she learnt the skills she felt she needed to survive in a cold, hard, clinical institution. She learnt to push. She learnt to shove. She learnt to fight. And she learnt to grab as much as she could for herself and shove it into her gob before anyone could come along and take it away from her.

In the light of her story, suddenly everything made sense. Evonne at last understood Rita's alienation, her anger, her strange, abnormal behaviour. Evonne understood Rita. And Rita knew Evonne understood.

Evonne and Rita became dear friends. When they talked, they laughed and cried. And after they laughed and cried, they danced. Now not many people I know dance in coffee shops; in Brisbane it's cool to dance in nightclubs, but it's not cool to dance in coffee shops. But after Evonne and Rita had bonded, Rita would often ask Evonne to dance with her round the tables and chairs of the Café Babylon. And though the customers found it rather strange, they didn't complain—as long as they got to eat their cheesecake in peace.

In the context of their friendship, Rita began to make some small but significant changes. The one I noticed was that she began to bum two cigarettes, rather than one, from passers-by. When questioned as to why she wanted two cigarettes, Rita replied, 'I want one for me and one for my friend Evonne.' This was the first sign I had ever seen of Rita showing care for anyone other than herself—and it was a beautiful moment to behold.

Over the next few years Evonne and Rita spent a lot of time together, not a little of it drinking coffee, eating cheesecake and smoking the cigarettes they cadged. But their chats, though casual, were anything but idle. Through their conversations Rita reclaimed her soul. As their relationship bloomed, Rita seemed to blossom too. She remembered songs from her youth, and she recovered her capacity to smile once again in her old age. She didn't do it often. She didn't want to overdo it. But when Rita did smile, it was as if Louis Armstrong had struck up the band playing 'It's a Wonderful World'.

One day, Rita had a stroke and was taken to hospital. Evonne was notified, and she and Navi rushed to Rita's ward. When they arrived, they were informed that the stroke had caused major damage and that Rita was already brain dead. The doctor told Evonne and Navi that they might as well go home, since nothing more could be done for Rita except to turn off the life support machine and let her pass away. Evonne and Navi said they understood the situation, but they could not go home and leave Rita in hospital, alone, as she had been before. They said Rita was their friend, and if she was going to die, they were going to make sure she did not die alone. So Evonne stood on one side of the bed and Navi stood on the other, and they held Rita's hands till she died.

A few months after the funeral, Evonne and I went for coffee and cheesecake at the Café Babylon for old times' sake. As we walked in, the waitress greeted Evonne like a long lost friend. Evonne introduced me to her. Then the waitress said something I will never forget. She said, 'It's so nice to see Evonne again. We miss her so much. When she used to come here regularly we loved it, because she used to bring her grandmother.'

Grandmother? The waitress must have thought that Rita was my daughter's grandmother! Obviously Evonne had related to Rita with such reverence that everyone in the café believed that Rita was actually a respected elderly member of our family.

And so, I guess, she was.

Lego and Life

Kim Hawtrey

In January 2001 the Powerhouse Museum in Sydney hosted a huge Lego exhibition. It was school holidays and I decided to take the kids to see what was on offer. One Saturday morning we piled into the car and off we went.

Everybody loves Lego, the toy building blocks that 'click' together to make structures. You can imagine how thousands of eyes lit up when the multitudes walked into the exhibition space at the Museum that day. And that was just the parents! The kids went crazy.

It was a feast for all ages, with brilliant scale models of pirate and space ships, even whole cities, complete with working lights and mechanical moving parts and each comprising thousands of Lego bricks. There was even a full size model of Darth Vader. We found out some interesting facts too: invented by a Dane called Mr Lego, these brightly coloured building blocks are Denmark's biggest export earner.

It was an interactive exhibit, and for some this was the best part. There were tables full of Lego bits and anyone could have a go at building something. Some of these construction spots featured 'special effects'. One of these was an Earthquake Platform. The table sat motionless much of the time, but every now and then it would erupt into a violent shaking motion. The tabletop had been wired to wobble every few minutes, to simulate an 'earthquake' and test the structures people had built upon it.

I stood and watched as a boy built a tower. His mother was with him. Up went the tower, higher and higher, as the kid—full of enthusiasm—applied all his engineering skills to the construction. Green, yellow, blue and red bricks. An ingenious design. Before long, it was taller than the boy himself.

Then, all of a sudden, the table base vibrated. Disaster struck: down came the tower, Lego cascading everywhere and scattering across the floor. The whole structure had collapsed. Nothing remained.

'You need a better foundation next time,' said the mother to her unhappy son.

It reminded me of a story Jesus told in Matthew chapter 7. There was a wise man who built his house on the rock. The rain came down, the floods rose and the winds blew and beat against that house. Yet it did not fall, because it had its foundation on rock.

Another man, whom Jesus described as foolish, built his

house on sand. The rain came down, the floods rose and the winds blew and beat against that house, and it fell with a great crash.

Finishing his story, Jesus concluded: *'Therefore everyone who hears these words of mine and puts them into practice is like a wise man who built his house on the rock. But everyone who hears these words of mine and does not put them into practice is like a foolish man who built his house on sand.'*

Life is a lot like that Lego table. Things seems to go pretty steadily much of the time, and it is easy to be fooled into a sense of complacency. But one day the earthquake will come: the judgment day when Jesus exposes the sins of men and women (Matthew 25:31–32).

On that day, we will need a firm Foundation: Jesus and his Word, the Bible, believed and acted upon in our life.

Doughnuts

Philip Baker

It is true that life and circumstances can have radically different interpretations, and sometimes we experience a cerebral jolt when we cross over what is now referred to as a 'paradigm shift'. This is where what we believed to be the case gets turned on its head.

The best example I have heard of this is the story of a man—we'll call him Fred—who was waiting for a flight in a busy airport somewhere in the world.

Fred decided to buy a bag of doughnuts while he was waiting for his boarding call. He purchased the doughnuts and went to a table, placed the bag of doughnuts on the table and then realised he would also like a cup of coffee. Fred returned to the counter, grabbed a coffee and came back to his table, only to find another traveller sitting at the same table. The cafeteria was reasonably busy and so he thought nothing of it. He had a sip of coffee, reached his hand into the bag of doughnuts and took one out.

The man sitting the other side of the table looked up and smiled, and then he too put his hand into the bag of doughnuts and took one out himself.

Fred could hardly believe his eyes. Here was a complete stranger helping himself, without even asking. Fred gave him one of those withering looks and went back to reading the newspaper and sipping his coffee.

After a while, Fred took another doughnut. This time, again, the other man reached in and took one as well. Fred bit his lip. He was about to say something, but as he was composing himself, an airport loud speaker announced a certain flight that was boarding, upon which the rude visitor at the table jumped up. He reached his hand one more time into the doughnut bag, took out the final doughnut, smiled at Fred, broke the doughnut in half and gave Fred one piece before walking off.

Fred was stunned. All he could do was sit there marvelling at the audacity of the man.

Soon it was time for Fred's plane to leave. He got up, picked up his coat and noticed that under the coat was a bag. He pulled it out. It was a bag of doughnuts.

Suddenly in a flash he grasped that this was his bag of doughnuts. As the wheels slowly turned, Fred realised that the man he had accused of eating his doughnuts was in fact innocent. The reality was that Fred had been eating his!

God As Business Partner

Gordon Moyes

Many people think that praying and refusing to worry about practical problems won't make any difference. Praying about *spiritual* problems, yes. But praying about practical problems, like meeting an impossible mortgage, finding the spare wheel not flat, or hoping the mobile phone you left on a city seat has not been pinched, no. That would be a waste of time.

Not to the bloke I met in Western Australia.

John Bridge was a contractor hauling clay for a brick-making company. But his equipment was old and deteriorating, needing attention beyond his means. His bank resources ran out, his profitability declined, and the fierce competitive nature of his area of work meant that he could not meet his obligations. He was $80,000 in debt, and the Monier Brick Company was unwilling to back him into the future.

At that point, when the whole of his life seemed to be tumbling in, John Bridge changed his attitude to worry.

He had been full of anxiety, skimping and scraping at every point, looking for short-cuts to make as much money as he could to keep his business afloat. But then John read a famous book, *Mover of Men and Mountains* by R. G. LeTournier, the world's greatest earthmoving equipment manufacturer. LeTournier told of taking God as his partner in business, and John decided to do the same.

He made four rules. Rule 1: He would not cheat for a single cent. He would pay all his road taxes. He would make sure he dealt honestly with everybody. Rule 2: If God wanted him to go out of business, he would willingly go out of business. Rule 3: He would not try to drum up work as before, but would allow God to open up the way for him. Rule 4: He would give to God a tenth of everything he earned, for God's work and service.

A month later, Monier phoned him. The company had never ordered more than 30,000 tons of clay a year from him. Now they said, 'We have a new development under way. Can you deliver 50,000 tons immediately?' He could and did.

As he was finalising delivery, they asked, 'Can you do another 10,000 tons?' And as he finalised the second order, Monier's other major supplier closed down and there was an order for another 20,000 tons.

At this point another problem confronted John. His pit ran out of clay. But he prayed about it and refused to worry. In order to get more, he had to dig further up the hill. He thought the location would not provide suitable clay, but when he took off the overburden, he discovered that the clay went down 60 feet—the greatest depth of good quality brick clay he had ever discovered. From there he took 120,000 tons for Monier.

Then there was another problem: he could take out clay only when the weather was dry. Once winter came he could not get the clay out. But he refused to worry about it—that was God's problem. And it just so happened that the year John made God his business partner turned out to be the driest year on record. He took out more clay. That year he made a profit and paid off all his debts.

John then bought two road trains, huge prime movers that pulled four or five sections, used for outback transport. With these, he would be able to carry cattle during the winter. He made a greater profit the following year.

Today, Bridge Contractors cross the nation, operating especially in Western Australia, Queensland and the west of New South Wales. When John told me about this, I asked: 'What changed your mind?' He quoted a verse from the Bible:

Be concerned above everything else with the Kingdom of God and with what he requires of you, and he will provide you with all these other things. So do not worry about tomorrow. (Matthew 6:33–34, TEV)

A Canticle for Catherine

Sue Duggan

Having children changes your life and everything in it forever. Half of me thinks that anybody considering becoming a parent should undergo a mandatory training course that at least equals aeronautical engineering or neurosurgery in its intensity. The other half of me knows that it wouldn't help a bit.

She first let us know that she was about to enter the world on the stroke of midnight. Just as the clock ticked over into her dad's birthday. If we had known her as well then as we do now, we would have known to expect her at precisely that moment. Catherine likes to drain every last drop out of life.

Despite some turbulence before touchdown, she landed unscathed in my arms around mid-morning. She passed all her tests with flying colours and impressed everyone with her alertness. With masses of black hair and skin like porcelain, she looked just like a china doll. The nurses assured me that, at a little less than 3 kilos, she was petite, not underweight as I feared.

As it turned out, our little banana in pyjamas was *very* tricky indeed. In hospital she got great press for being the snooziest baby in the nursery. We presumed that this was a transferable skill, something she would be proud to take home with her. We were wrong. From the moment she came home to her adoring audience and entered her balloon-filled nursery, she did not sleep very much at all.

I didn't worry too much about it at first, but as I got less and less sleep, I worried in exponential proportion to my sleep loss. I also worried because my already tiny bundle began to lose weight. Only a couple of hundred grams at each check-up, but by Christmas she was five weeks old and weighed less than her birth weight. The experts told us to supplement breastfeeding with some formula.

We bought every formula, bottle and teat on the market but none of them impressed our tiny connoisseur. She spat them back at us one at a time. We thought she was just fussy. Any person who believes that babies do not have much personality until they begin to speak needs to see our videos of the 'feeding frenzy'. I'm currently considering donating them to medical research. They might be useful in those preparation for parenthood classes in the 'How Not to Do It' section.

Underneath all my new mum bravado, I was sure something way beyond terrible was wrong with my baby. The more I expressed my fears, the more the experts hinted that possibly there was nothing wrong with Catherine and maybe I just needed to relax. Eventually I began to think I must be overreacting.

New Year's Eve was not an especially hot day, but Catherine got very sweaty. She had little beads of perspiration all over her body. She was in a great mood, but still she did not want to drink. We gave her a cool bath after which she vomited. It being New Year's Eve, we decided to take her to a doctor while there was still one easily available. The doctor examined her carefully and told us that he couldn't find anything wrong. On the way out the door, he asked who was doing her surgery.

It was obvious that we had no idea what he meant. We went back inside and he told us. Catherine was experiencing heart failure. He assumed that we already knew about it, so when he said there was nothing wrong he meant there was nothing *else* wrong! She had what he thought was a sizeable hole in her heart. The lack of sleep, inability to suck a bottle, sweatiness and even her beautiful porcelain skin were all symptoms. He told us that she would need to have open-heart surgery. He explained as much as he could and then asked us if we had any questions. We didn't. We were too stunned to think.

That night we didn't celebrate New Year's Eve. We sat looking at each other and at our baby.

I didn't go to bed. It was some weeks before I learned that

heart failure is a medical term that means the heart is not working efficiently. That night, I believed it was synonymous with heart attack. I was suddenly very afraid that Catherine was going to die while I slept. I sat by her cradle at the end of our bed and placed my little finger in her hand. I felt powerless. Overwhelmed. Our lives were so full of her. In five short weeks, she had become the centre of our universe.

I tried to talk to her as I sat on the floor, but I could not think of a word to describe how much I loved her that wasn't either too small or overused. At that moment, I could easily have given my life in exchange for hers. I would have done anything to make her better. I felt blessed, terrified and guilty all at once. Blessed because I knew that the same guy who designed the entire universe gave Catherine to us. Terrified at the thought of losing her. And guilty because I thought I should have known.

As every emotion in the book vied to be top dog, a wave of fear overshadowed everything else. What happens if she dies and she doesn't know how much I love her?

I began to pray: 'Lord, heal her, protect her.' Soon, however, I caught myself saying other things.

'Lord, how could you? . . . I can't believe you let this happen to me . . . Call yourself omniscient? Where were you when this happened? . . . You know me, Lord, and you know I'm no Abraham, so don't even think of asking me to give her back . . . God, I am so angry with you! Where are you now, because I can't feel you? I know there's probably a war on in Botswana or somewhere, but I need you here in the suburbs.'

I fell asleep berating the only person who really had a handle on this mess.

I woke up cold and stiff. Catherine was awake and blowing bubbles at me from her cot. She looked perfect. As another rush of emotions hit, I felt a physical pain in my heart. Love or heartache, I was not sure.

I remembered then the serve that I sent skyward before falling asleep.

'Oh, no! Lord, I'm sorry. You must get this all the time. I'm sorry about the Abraham stuff, but you know it's all true. I'm a wimp. I'm sorry for taking it all out on you; that's not fair. I know you're not responsible for this. I was angry. I *am* angry.'

Moments later I was sure I heard a voice. 'It's okay, I know,' it seemed to say. 'I love you at least as much as you love Catherine.'

From that moment I had a feeling that things were going to be all right. Over the next few years there were so many horrible, scary days, and I thought about that night many times. Some days it was the only thing that got me through.

Catherine is now a healthy, vibrant nine-year-old. She has an infectious sense of humour and plans to be a clown and a part-time opera singer when she grows up. First, though, she is going to have four children. Their dad, who will be an artist, will take care of them at night when Catherine does concerts in the city.

Narrabeen's Story

Mal Garvin

Narrabeen Beach, 24 kilometres north of Sydney, is an unbroken stretch of golden sand, now gradually recovering from pollutants. This stretch of sand is pounded by Pacific breakers and ends where the mouth of a small lake empties into the ocean. Today two bridges cross that lake, and between them, in the holiday season, hundreds of campers can be seen.

In the early days of white settlement, this land was heavily wooded. The Aboriginal tribe of the area was blessed with wonderful fishing and hunting grounds. It was in this setting 185 years ago that momentous events took place. While the detail of what happened is debated, the general outline is clear.

The first white man to live in the area was Captain Ian Reynolds, who came out with the First Fleet. After retiring from the military, Reynolds built a home for himself and his family in that region. He was very friendly with a group of

Aboriginals who lived nearby, and after some time became a special friend to their chief, Yowal.

Narrabeen was Yowal's daughter—a beautiful, gentle-hearted Aboriginal, deeply related to the Australian bush that the Creator God had given to her people. As a small girl she had sat around the campfire, hearing stories of the white men and their strange ways. She had heard of big boats; of sticks that made loud noises and hurt; of the mistreatment of her people by white men.

She had seen the fear and anger reflected in the faces of members of her tribe, and she too had been afraid.

On the other hand, she had also watched these white men landing on the beaches, doing some fishing and even throwing water at each other in play. This made her wonder if they were as evil as some of the men of the tribe said. With the coming of Captain Reynolds, her fears tended to subside.

One day some news came that stirred up her fear anew. 'Bolters'—desperate escaped convicts—were roaming the bush. This particular group was led by a criminal and sociopath dubbed 'Big Mick'.

Amazingly enough, Narrabeen stumbled on the camp of these men, and her grasp of English was sufficient for her to understand that they were plotting to kill Captain Reynolds. It seems that in the past Reynolds had ordered Big Mick to be flogged after he had attempted to lead a convict mutiny.

Now in revenge Mick planned to kill every member of the pioneer household.

Narrabeen's heart must have pounded with the knowledge that if she were discovered, she would certainly die. Shadow-like, she crept away from the grim discussion.

It was this point of decision that wrote Narrabeen into history. No doubt a part of her simply wanted to leave the white man to his own madness and to withdraw more deeply into the bush with her own people. But something larger than the desire to protect her own territory took hold of her. Something within her cared more about others than her own safety.

She sped to her father Yowal, who quickly made his way to the Reynolds homestead to warn the white people. At the same time he sent her out of the safety of her own bush neighbourhood to seek help in the alien city of Sydney.

Having been warned, Reynolds and his family barricaded themselves in and took up arms. Mrs Reynolds put her baby into its cot and took her place alongside her husband and their thirteen-year-old son, each with a rifle.

Meanwhile, Narrabeen pushed swiftly through twenty miles of bush to Sydney. Here she made herself known to the authorities, who were persuaded to take her story seriously and were goaded into action. With a detachment of soldiers from the garrison, no doubt many of whom wondered what kind of a wild-goose chase they were going on, she returned to her home. They arrived too late to save the Reynolds family, but in time to capture Big Mick and his gang.

It would have been so easy for this young woman to have simply withdrawn and focused on preserving herself and her people. But in Narrabeen's story, as in other stories about human beings who have cared in a special way, God gives us a glimpse of who he is, and of what we're called to be—generous and compassionate.

The Idol Busyness of Suburbia

Phillip Jensen

Julie was so excited. Her brother was finally coming to an evangelistic meeting. For years she had been praying for him, longing that he might come to the Saviour that she knew so well.

They had grown up going to Sunday school and the youth group at church. But as they moved into adulthood, she had come to put her trust in Christ while he had followed his father's footsteps away from Christ.

They had remained good friends as siblings but rarely had much time to see each other. Life got busy with career, marriage and children. Although they lived in the same region of Sydney, it was not the same suburb, and their children went to different schools.

From time to time Julie had invited Robert to different Christian meetings, and although he was never offended or upset by the invitations, he just never made it. Sometimes he would be there for Christmas at the old family church when they were having lunch with their parents. Sometimes he would be at a family wedding or funeral where something of the gospel was expressed. But this time he was coming to an out and out evangelistic meeting—and Julie was thrilled.

The night went very well. The meeting was smoothly organised. Outsiders were not put off by those embarrassing and irrelevant Christian subcultural activities—like amplifier breakdowns or Christian in-jokes. But best of all, the speaker, in a warm, clear, intelligent and compelling way, made the gospel of Jesus as attractive as Julie had ever heard it. It is so wonderful when people faithfully explain the wonder of our Saviour's love in his death for us.

'Surely,' Julie thought, 'Rob must get the message this time.'

It was not hard on the way home to discuss the speaker's message. He had made it perfectly clear and Rob was obviously moved by it. He wanted to talk about it. Yes, he believed it was true. Yes, he really thought that he should do something about it. Yes, he had always known it was true. And yes, he had always loved his sister's clear commitment to Christ.

But—and this was a big but—he was pretty busy at the moment.

He had just bought the new house, and the mortgage was pretty high, and the promotion at work was very timely because it brought more pay but it did involve more work and a lot more travel and longer hours. Then there were the kids.

With Bill going to a different high school from Fiona it meant that there were three different schools for four children, and their sporting commitments on Sunday morning meant church-going was out of the question, and ... and ...

It is strange how relevant to today the parables of Jesus are. The parable of the great banquet, in which a variety of people are invited to the feast of the kingdom of God but refuse to come (Luke 14:16–24), readily came to mind when I heard of Julie's disappointment over her brother. Like the rest of Scripture, it does not require all that much recontextualising because it is about the basic human condition.

Our sinfulness is not usually expressed in degenerate behaviour but in the stupidity of our godless priorities. We know the truth but live the lie, denying ourselves the pleasure of God's company for the idol busyness of suburbia.

Names in this story have been changed.

Destination: Anywhere

Colin Buchanan

As the little plane climbed above the patchwork of New England paddocks, I got chatting to fellow musician Mal about a recent series of shows he had done in Asia. He'd found the social fabric of Asian society fascinating. Talk of comparative culture turned to comparative religion and in turn to Mal's Eastern-flavoured philosophy of life.

'I believe you've got to contribute to your society for good. You can't be a mongrel—you have to make your overall goal one that benefits others. I'm not so sure there's a personal God, just a prevailing energy for good . . .' Such was the world according to Mal. Probably no God. Focus on the good within. East is Best.

I contended that if there was a God, goddess or gods, by definition they would exist outside the created order, and should he, she or they wish us lot to know anything about him, her or themselves, they'd need to reveal such information to us mere mortals. 'Our dilemma is the diversity of conclusions people draw from the evidence around them. From Buddha to Mohammed to Mal to Brad to the One I admit I've staked my life on, Jesus Christ—there are so many different versions of "The Answer". How can we be sure who's got it right—or wrong?'

'But there's a different reality for all of us,' said Mal. 'They all ultimately serve the same purpose.'

'I still marvel that reasonable, educated people can really go for that one, Mal. It's just New Age apathy. It's a wholemeal, unbleached, '90s, politically correct "she'll be right".' Mal chuckled. 'And my problem with that view is that we just don't live the rest of our lives like that. We got on this plane because we believed it would take us safely to Sydney. We drive with our eyes open. We don't deliberately put our hands into boiling water. I can't see why the reason so essential for living in the physical world should be abandoned when it comes to the spiritual world. Marx was an atheist, Jesus Christ wasn't. They contradict each other. They can't both be right.'

'Marx and Jesus were both basically on about equality and social justice,' Mal responded.

'Granted, Jesus loved the unlovely, the unclean, the outcast. But he was on about something much bigger. His first words recorded in Mark's Gospel weren't "Feed the poor" but "Repent and believe, for the kingdom of God is near." He was on about reconciling human beings to God. I think a lot of people have an impression of Jesus without ever reading the historical documents with an open mind.'

We talked about the confronting nature of the historical Jesus, the historicity of the New Testament and how poorly some of the other major alternatives stacked up in comparison. We considered the radical nature of Jesus' death and subsequent resurrection—and the compelling evidence that it really happened. We had a stimulating, warm and satisfying discussion. We covered a lot of territory. And it wasn't long before we were 100 kilometres to the north of Sydney being told to stow our hand luggage.

Mal found himself restating his original philosophy. 'But I believe there's basically a big scale and our aim is to make the good of our lives outweigh the bad. Work for the collective good and it'll all work out.'

'Mal, the problem is we don't even live up to our own standards. I don't live up to yours—we can't. Forget any divine standards, we can't even live up to our own. The scales keep tipping the wrong way.'

Mal said nothing—he could see the problem.

'Let me put your philosophy another way . . .' I thought I'd heard the essence of Mal's words before.' "Love the Lord your God with all your heart and soul and mind and strength, and love your neighbour as yourself." That's God's standard. And we fail miserably.'

Less than a minute to touchdown.

'I find enormous comfort in Christianity's concept of forgiveness,' I continued. 'Your philosophy is based on your own flawed performance. Christianity is based on Jesus' perfect performance. No matter what, I can know that I'm forgiven. My relationship with God is rock solid.'

There was a thump as our plane connected with the tarmac. Mal was gazing out the window. 'That is a powerful concept,' he said.

Our journey, and our conversation, was at an end. Strangely, it was Mal's final's words that were ringing in my ears. Forgiveness *is* such a powerful concept. And it's a reality for all who call on the name of Jesus Christ. Without knowing it, Mal had refocused my mind on the wonder of the gospel. I pray that someday soon he might marvel at it for himself.

The Party Dress

Angela Eynaud

Money was tight in our house when I was growing up. All our appliances were old, often second-hand. From the car to the mower, money was only spent on maintenance when something broke down.

Mum's sewing machine was a classic. It chewed and looped more than it sewed, but with that unreliable, clanking monster my mother produced beautiful clothes for her children. My sisters had gorgeous frocks in Swiss voile, velvet and hailspot muslin, pintucked, smocked or embroidered. Each one was a work of painstaking love.

Mum was creative, with an eye for style and beauty, but she was no dressmaker. Bodices were sewn on upside down, unpicked and sewn on again. Sleeves were put on inside out, unpicked and put on again. Zips were inserted three times before they finally went in straight, up the right way and facing out. By the time each garment was completed, it would have gone through a series of metamorphoses. The end result was unfailingly splendid.

On the night before my grade four end-of-year party, my new dress was still in a pile of cut-out pattern pieces. That was another thing about my mum. She was talented but disorganised. 'Never fear,' I was told, 'it's only a few hours' work. I promise your dress will be finished in the morning.'

Halfway through the first seam, however, there was a sickening crunch. The needle snapped and the fabric of my new party dress was pulled down into the machine's workings, where it jammed fast.

It was the 1960s. The term 'party dress' meant something back then. Each girl owned one special dress for birthday parties. We'd arrive at parties spotless, starched and frilly, the toes of our party shoes freshly whitened. Some would have had their hair bound in rag curls overnight.

There were no bouncing castles back then. It was the time of Chocolate Crackles, ice cream and jelly, drop-the-hanky and musical chairs. Not to have a party dress was a social disaster. I went to bed anxiously eyeing my mother settling down on the couch with a needle and thread.

In the morning my new party dress was hanging completed on the back of my door. Mum was in the kitchen with red-rimmed eyes. She had sat up all night and sewn every stitch by hand. My mum had kept her promise.

I remember telling two ladies at church what mum had done, showing them my new dress. I was surprised by their reaction. They were not impressed at all but found her extraordinary effort amusing, even eccentric. Patronising advice was offered about the better economy of maintaining household appliances. They cried out over the absurdity of persevering simply because a promise had been made to a child. Finally the dress was examined and found wanting because the inferior stitching was already beginning to unravel.

In the eyes of more organised, more practical people, my mother's labour of love appeared absurd. Only in my heart was she a hero; among the Ladies' Guild she was a fool. According to these purse-lipped matrons, love should be measured out in careful doses equal to the occasion. Those who are lavish with love, who waste it on undeserving cases, are worthy of ridicule.

I recognised the same attitude when I grew older and learned of a Saviour who claimed to be a king but who died naked on a cross because of his prodigal love for an undeserving people. People jeered at him too.

Neil's Spiritual U-turn

Philip Johnson

I met Neil Saintilan in Victoria Park outside the grounds of Sydney University. He was a first year student in science and geography, and at the moment when I interrupted him, Neil was sitting on a grassy slope meditating. He was tall with a slender build, blond-haired and quite cheery.

I was accompanied by David, and we were participants in a campus ministry known as Student Life. Student Life is the Australian version of the famous US-based ministry Campus Crusade for Christ. True to the form of Student Life, we were using our free time to talk to fellow students about Jesus.

Neil was eager to talk with us because he was a keen adept of meditation. In his high school days, he began to awaken to spiritual sensitivities within himself and in the world around him. His scholastic interests in geography and biology dovetailed neatly with his enthralment with the beauty of the natural world. He read the romantic poets like Wordsworth, who evoked deep yearnings in him for sublime feelings and a sense of joy, all interfused with nature. As a self-reflective teenager, Neil questioned the materialist lifestyle of his peers and family. He discerned that neither he nor the natural world were merely physical entities. He intuited a spiritual dimension both in reality at large and within himself that cried out for expression and fulfilment.

Towards the end of high school, Neil discovered some books by eastern mystics and gurus. He stumbled onto the writings of the first modern Hindu missionary to the West, Swami Vivekananda (1863–1902), and those of the founder of the Hare Krishna movement, Swami Prabhupada. Neil was very impressed by what he read. He understood from Vivekananda that the soul was real, eternal and divine. The journey through this life was all about overcoming a perceived separation from God. This could be attained by being detached from the mundane things of life. From Prabhupada he discovered the need for a spiritual discipline to assist him in the quest for a purified, holy consciousness.

Along with the practical discipline of daily meditation, Neil also aligned the routines of his daily life with the ethical precepts that these Swamis expounded. What nailed things even more for Neil was the eminent support given to these antique Hindu insights in the book *The Tao of Physics*, written by the Austrian physicist Fritjof Capra. Capra found parallels between quantum physics, with its models about matter and energy at a sub-atomic level, and the metaphysical views of Hindu and Taoist belief.

The promise of reunion with God was exciting, so Neil embarked on his own spiritual pathway using daily meditation exercises as the means of reaching purity and reunion with God. He experienced the real and positive benefits that meditation brings, such as a sense of calm, serenity and deep relaxation. These valuable and positive effects spurred Neil on to explore the nature of consciousness and the pursuit of God.

But as an adept of this pathway soon discovers, the attempt to attain the promise of union with God is fraught with many struggles and disappointments. Neil realised after two years of ardent meditation and study that he was far from overcoming his moral impurities, and God seemed elusive and remote. He had gained some useful and meaningful insights into himself and his personality, and could clearly see that the creation had a purpose. However, the tantalising promise seemed unattainable, and he sensed some inner frustration at being impotent to find fulfilment in his pathway.

When David and I met Neil he had spent two years as an avid meditator. David kindly let me do much of the sharing about Jesus with Neil. We spent about two hours talking about God and the way of Jesus. Neil felt that Christians were an arrogant lot, and assumed that Christianity was an inferior pathway because of its emphasis on doctrines and the events of Jesus' life. He raised some serious questions such as why a good God would tolerate evil, the impossibility of reconciling the theory of evolution with the creation story, and the possibility of historical errors in the Bible.

We had some good dialogue on these questions, and as our time was drawing to a close, I challenged him. As Neil evidenced a passion in searching for spiritual nourishment, I asked him if he would be willing to read some materials that addressed the kinds of questions he had raised. He said he would, so two days later I passed on to him five books as a gift. A few days later he posted me a note saying that he appreciated my gift, and especially so because it arrived the day before his birthday. He also wrote that in the light of my actions he was withdrawing his criticism about arrogant Christians.

I met up with Neil a few days later and he told me he had devoured the books. He wanted to know more, so we spent three more hours talking about some pretty deep matters. I passed on to him a Christian book that responded to Buddhism and gave him two spiritual autobiographies. The following week he handed the three books back having read them. The book on Buddhism had missed the mark for him, but the autobiographies impressed him. We chatted for two more hours and then parted, with Neil obviously feeling challenged but far from persuaded.

I did not see Neil for a couple of months, but eventually

bumped into him a few times travelling home on the train. We had further brief conversations. Around this time Neil began to discover that some of his closest friends at university either were long-standing believers or had recently become Christians. These friends began to consolidate what I had started to share with Neil. He accompanied them to a few meetings of the Navigators and the Evangelical Union and continued to talk with them. He started to read bits of the Bible too.

Certain teachings began to take hold in Neil's thoughts. He was struck by the sense of God's holiness and the evil and moral failings we humans are prone to. He started to see that moral failure was not just something that could be overcome by self-effort; rather, it was the absolute state of humanity. Neil recognised that his own efforts at tackling his imperfect nature and errant behaviour were disqualified in God's sight. He then understood that God alone could provide the solution through Jesus.

Neil found it a colossal struggle to acknowledge that his own efforts to reach God were futile and that he had to have a change of mind. A spiritual U-turn was needed. About one year after I first spoke to him, Neil read a book by the Australian evangelist John Chapman, *A Fresh Start*. In it he found a prayer for forgiveness, and Neil's spiritual U-turn began immediately as he repented of his own ways and acknowledged that only God could forgive and transform him forever.

Some eighteen years have passed since then and Neil is still a disciple of Jesus. He has studied at Moore Theological College, is happily married and actively participates in his local church. He is also an expert on the ecology of mangroves, wetlands and swamps, and teaches in this discipline. I have had the privilege of observing Neil share his story with others and been honoured to speak at his church.

Neil's story remains an encouraging reminder to me that conversations with seeming strangers about Jesus can and often do bear fruit that lasts forever.

The Widow's Mite

Jonathan Krause

Sitting across from the offering box, he was observing how the crowd tossed money in for the collection. Many of the rich were making large contributions. One poor widow came up and put in two small coins—a measly two cents. Jesus called his disciples over and said, 'The truth is that this poor widow gave more to the collection than all the others put together. All the others gave what they'll never miss; she gave extravagantly what she couldn't afford—she gave her all.' (Mark 12:41–44, THE MESSAGE)

Kalaboli Mondal is an old, old lady. She is bent way to the ground, and her face has seen a thousand lifetimes. She wears a light aqua-colour sari, old and worn like its wearer, but with beauty still shining through.

When we meet, Kalaboli takes my hand in both of hers, clasps it tight, and then smiles up at me with crystal clear eyes. Her friendliness makes me feel instantly comfortable, right at home in the dust outside the mud hut where she lives. I've heard a story about Kalaboli I can barely believe.

In Bangladesh they do a '20 Hour Famine' to raise money for needy children. Mostly it is World Vision workers who fast, and the community they serve who support them. In Hariampur, where Kalaboli lives, the people are very poor, and floods have driven many from their land into Dhaka in search of work. Yet this community, so poor, raised 16,000 taka ($500) to help needy children.

Kalaboli is eighty-five years old, a widow, and she begs to survive. She tells me: 'I have nothing to do now, but I used to fry rice to sell. Sometimes I collect food from my son's house. I eat there. Or if people offer me food, I will survive.'

When the '20 Hour Famine' was promoted, Kalaboli came to World Vision and said she wanted to give her support. 'I am only able to give 5 taka for the poor and destitute. I am a beggar, but would you receive my donation?'

Kalaboli's gift of 5 taka (15 cents) was all the money she had.

When I ask her why she, who had so little, was willing to give, she says: 'I have seen your World Vision people doing so many good things in this area, and I believe this small amount of money will be properly used for the poor and destitute people.'

I have no words to respond to such generosity. I try to communicate my thanks to Kalaboli by touching her hands again, but she just smiles and asks me to stay, and she will prepare lunch for me. Then she kneels to the ground and touches both my feet in the Bangladeshi sign of respect.

I've never felt so undeserving. This woman's donation of a few cents was worth more than the largest donation I've ever seen.

And that's a lesson for me. So often in our culture we celebrate only the big achievements—the great sporting events, the mega-movie stars, the Top 10 money-making entrepreneurs. And in World Vision, where I work, sometimes we fall into the trap of only acknowledging the 'major' gifts, whether of money or of service. But really we need to be celebrating all the so-called little gifts from the so-called 'little people'— those who give extravagantly, who give all they have, simply because they care.

Kalaboli is an old lady. A widow. A beggar. She owns a sari and that's about all. Yet the little she had, she gave. With a willing heart and a smile of love. She is the one who deserves the respect. She is the one whose feet should be kissed.

Photos, Faith and Finances

Steve Grace

Winter mist had settled in over the small timber town of Oberon in the Blue Mountains. Our concert at the local RSL was a night best forgotten. The crowd was small, the atmosphere as cold as the temperature outside. Some local churches had boycotted the event because of the venue. Instead of seeing the performance as an opportunity to present the gospel to the community, they were threatened by the thought of a Christian concert in a place filled with cigarette smoke, poker machines and alcohol.

I was saddened by the rows of empty seats but appreciated the support of the small church that had invited the band to come. Ron Hartland and his family had prayed for months for this night, believing that many people in the town would be encouraged.

We loaded the truck in the bitter cold and made our way quietly to the Hartlands' home. I remember asking myself as we followed their car in the fog, 'Lord, why did we come here? What was this night all about? All that effort and nothing to show for it.' Few people, little response—and I knew that after expenses we would probably come away with just $200 from the event. It was easy to justify my negativity.

Over hot coffee and Vegemite on toast we soon relaxed and warmed up around the living room fire. I noticed a photo album on the table and began browsing through pictures of the Hartland family's recent missions trip to Vanuatu in the South Pacific. Images of pristine coral beaches, island villages, ocean canoes and friendly, smiling faces took me far away from the present.

I turned the page and was confronted with a most disturbing picture. It showed a young boy with a horribly deformed leg leaning on a walking stick. In fact, there were a number of photographs, including some very graphic close-ups.

I turned to Ron for an explanation. His eyes welled with tears of compassion.

The boy was Alfred, a nine year old whose leg had been crushed by a falling tree when he was five. His parents lived on an outer island where there were no medical services. The village could not even afford the fuel to get the injured boy to the hospital on the main island, so they cared for him in the village as best they could. His leg had been broken in many places and eventually had healed into the mangled, deformed state shown in the photographs.

Alfred was destined to spend his life as a cripple. He would never kick a soccer ball with his friends on the village field, never spearfish from the offshore coral reefs, never run and never fully experience the joy and adventure of his youth. Yet in spite of his tragic circumstances, every photograph showed Alfred with a bright, beaming smile.

Ron had taken the pictures in a desperate attempt to do something, anything for the crippled boy. I was filled with a strong conviction to see this young boy's life changed. Deeply disturbed by my selfish attitude regarding the poorly attended concert on that cold winter's night, I silently repented to the Lord.

Ron went on to tell me that he had shown the collection of photographs to some Christian doctors in Sydney. They were confident that a series of long and painful operations in Australia, costing some $9000 of surgical theatre time, would give the young boy a chance at a normal life. In faith the Hartlands had just opened a special bank account, believing that God would supply the funds needed for the airfares and operations.

I sat there on the lounge for an hour staring at the photographs while everyone slowly dragged themselves off to bed. How could we help a crippled kid in a poor island nation get healed from an accident that had happened years before? In those solemn moments, I realised we had not come to this town to do a big, impressive concert. God brought the team and me to this community to meet the Hartland family and be captivated by their love for a boy named Alfred.

It took a while to get to sleep that night. The next morning I jumped out of bed like a man inspired with a new mission. I asked Ron how much money they had in the account for Alfred. 'Nothing yet,' he replied. I grabbed the chequebook and wrote out a gift for $200—all that we had made the night before. I handed it to Ron and said, 'Well, here's the start. And there's more on the way!

'We'll share your vision for Alfred through the concerts,' I declared in faith. 'I know God wants us to be part of it.'

The next night in the city of Orange, the local high school hall was packed with over 750 people. Churches and youth groups had driven from towns throughout the region to attend the concert. It was an enthusiastic atmosphere. Many made decisions that night to trust God with their lives. I shared my story about the night before, the photo album and the boy called Alfred. I invited people to help him. And they did. People gave hundreds of dollars. The folks from the local Salvation Army were there, and they asked if they too could raise some funds. We drove out of Orange the next morning eager to get to the next town, and the next. We were on a mission.

Two weeks later I received an urgent phone call from Ron Hartland. 'Steve, stop telling people about Alfred! We've got too much money! More than enough!'

We laughed with grateful hearts. God had provided the funds through ordinary people.

Eight months later I had the privilege of meeting Alfred. His leg was in a cast. He came to my concert at the Cowra Civic Centre with the Hartland family. Miraculously, the doctors had been able to completely straighten his crippled leg with just one operation.

Today, he plays in the soccer team for his village in Vanuatu.

Doubts

Max Meyers

Max Meyers resigned from a successful and glamorous career as a pilot in the RAAF so he could join Missionary Aviation Fellowship (MAF). However, he struggled with doubts and questions about his decision . . .

I had always expected that my departure from military life would be like a wonderful graduation. I thought that these would be great days of confidence in God, of joyful assurance that I was walking the right path. Instead I found myself wondering where God was and why he didn't deal directly with my troubled heart and fill me with confident trust. I found myself wondering if I was even right to believe in a 'personal call' and if God really did have a plan for my life.

Alone in the car, I had cried out repeatedly to the One whom by this time I was almost convinced was a totally disinterested and non-hearing God. With deep emotion, I prayed,

'God, what am I going to do? Please help me . . . if you are there. I can't go on like this.'

There was no answer.

At the western end of Ballarat there is a memorial arch across the highway, a kind of mini 'Arch de Triumph'. I had passed under this arch many times.

As I approached, travelling at about sixty miles per hour, I noticed a man sitting at its base in the darkness. He stood to his feet and cocked his thumb at me. It was awfully late, about midnight, so I knew he really needed a ride.

I saw the plea in his face as I sped past. *Not tonight*, I thought. *I don't care how desperate you are. I don't want to talk with anyone.* If I had stopped, I could not have hidden from him the emotional upheaval that was taking place in my life. I didn't want to explain this to anyone, let alone a man trying to thumb a lift.

So I drove on.

It must have been thirty minutes later, and at least thirty or forty miles farther along the road, that I began to think a little differently. *Has God ever left me? Was it possible that the voices of doubt, self-pity and shame were shouting so loudly in my ears that I could not hear what God was saying?*

I had to acknowledge that was not only possible but likely.

Then the thought came to me. Although God hadn't used my friend the pastor to speak to me, there may be others. Suddenly I remembered the stranger standing by the arch. Maybe he was there, just for me.

No, that's a ludicrous idea. It's illogical. Ridiculous.

I drove on for a while thinking about him. Who was he? What would he have said to me had I stopped and picked him up? What would I have said to him? No, it was stupid to think that he could be a messenger to me. But slowly the conviction grew in my mind that this man could be of significance to me, that he could have been placed there by God, just for me, at this very moment.

No one saw me stop the car, turn around on the highway, and make my way back toward Ballarat. It was a crazy thing to do. The hitchhiker would, in all probability, be long since gone. But I drove all that way back. I had to do it.

And he was still there.

This time, of course, I was approaching from the opposite direction so he didn't even stand up. He didn't need a ride in the direction my car was headed. I drove through the arch, turned around, rolled down the window, and stopped by him.

'Want a lift?' I asked him.

I guess he couldn't understand why a car should appear out of the darkness from the west, turn around in front of him, and offer him a ride back in a westerly direction. His wariness was apparent. 'No, thanks. I'm wanting to go back there where you've come from.'

'Well, mate, that's where I'm going now. Come on, hop in. I'll take you home.'

We didn't say a word to each other for some time as I

drove toward Adelaide. I'm sure he was wondering exactly what was happening. I didn't want to talk with him anyway. I just wanted to know if he had something to say—from God!

As I watched him out of the corner of my eye, he sat quietly staring at the dashboard of the car. After a while I noticed a change in his demeanour. He was breathing deeply. I sensed tension, confusion. He sighed a loud sigh, a couple of times, as if something was really bothering him. Then, with a voice filled with emotion, he said to me, 'Mate, we haven't talked yet, but I simply have to ask you something. I don't know who you are or why you picked me up. Seems to me you were going the other way. I don't know if you can understand my question, let alone answer it, but I need to ask you something. It's terribly important to me just now.'

I didn't want questions from him. I wanted answers! But I told him to go ahead anyway.

'It may seem like a crazy question,' he said, 'but it's simply this.' He hesitated. 'Do you really believe in God? I have to know.'

I was totally startled by what he had said. Who on earth was this man? Driving back to the arch was more an act of desperation on my part than anything else. I was the needy one. From the emptiness of my store of faith I had nothing to offer him. After all, I was the one who stood in need of spiritual help and counsel. How could I, of all people, confirm the reality and presence of God to some stranger, and a hitchhiker at that?

Evasively I said, 'Why do you ask a question like that?'

'I'll have to tell you a story,' he said. 'It'll probably sound ridiculous, but I have to tell you.

'On Saturday I went by train to Melbourne to watch football,' he said. 'I met some friends there and after the game we went for a quick drink, but it turned out to be anything but quick. My friends and I drank long into the evening, well after the departure time of my train back home. I had no other option but to spend the night there. There's only one train a day on our line on the weekend. So this afternoon I went to the station in plenty of time to catch the Sunday train. And an amazing thing happened there.

'A bloke stood on the footpath preaching. I'm a country boy from Horsham, and street preachers would be a bit of a joke there. But something made me want to listen to him. He described my life exactly. Hopeless. Not a lot of direction. He spoke about God . . . and love. He said that God was the answer to my problems. He told me I could know God like a father. He used the word "lost" . . . exactly how I felt.

'It was time for the train,' he continued, 'but I couldn't walk away from this man. I had to listen, so I let the train go. What he was talking about was more important than going home.'

As my passenger went on with his story, he explained that he had never heard anything like this before. After the street preacher had finished, he had spoken with him personally, asking whether such an amazing story applied to him. And this time, face-to-face, he heard again the story of God's love, of forgiveness and . . . eternal life. He heard of a Saviour who died and rose again to draw even football fans to himself.

'I found myself, right there in the street with everybody around, repeating a prayer, the very first prayer of my life. I asked God to forgive me. I asked him to give me that new life I had just heard about,' he told me.

'This preacher bloke took me to meet his friends at a church, and speaking with them, I knew that something marvellous had happened to me. I came to Melbourne to watch a footy match and I had found God. Actually, God had found me. Mate, I have never felt anything like the feelings I had there.

'But I had to get home,' he said. 'I have to be at work in the morning. The people from the church drove me a number of miles out of town to thumb a ride home. It was quite a while before anyone stopped for me. I got as far as Ballarat a couple of hours ago. I've been sitting under that arch trying to get another ride.

'I gotta admit. Last night was amazing, but sitting there alone in the cold has been a bad, bad time. I've been turning over in my mind all that happened in Melbourne.

'But then I began to doubt.

'What really had happened? Could my life have been so totally changed through hearing a story and praying a prayer?

Who were those people? How do I know it's true? None of my family or friends believes this stuff. How am I going to tell them? Have I been hoodwinked or brainwashed by some religious nut?

'So, I've been sitting at the base of that arch arguing with myself and asking God to show himself to me. I'd almost decided to forget the whole thing. Maybe it was something weird that had happened and that should be forgotten. But I couldn't do it. It had been too real.'

He went on with his incredible story as the miles passed by.

'Finally,' he said, 'just before you came, in desperation I stood and cried out to God the second prayer of my life. "If you are real, God, please send someone to tell me. Please. Please."'

He looked across at me, pleading. 'So, do you think this is all crazy, or not? Whether you can answer my question or not, I have to ask it. Do you believe in God?'

Did I believe in God? This newborn believer, fresh in the knowledge of a salvation that was real but already under threat, was asking me to confirm the validity of his actions in Melbourne the previous evening. As his story unfolded, I had heard the voice of God speaking to me, answering the cries of my own soul, filling me with a new certainty of faith. This was a divine appointment—for me! I was totally reassured. My reassured heart said to me, 'Go on, you tell him. Tell him that God is utterly and completely trustworthy.'

And so I did.

'You've told me your story,' I then said to him. 'Now, I have to tell you mine. Yes, God is trustworthy. God is real. Even in the times of heart-wrenching doubts. In fact, he is here in this car. Right now. My doubts, your doubts, don't change him at all. And I've been brought here to tell you just that. He does love you. He is love. And last night he gave you the honour of knowing him personally.'

I went on to share with him my own terrible time of doubting. I told him of my need for someone to come into my life and bring me God's message of assurance. I told him that I believed he was that person. God had sent him to me . . .

A great and wonderful encounter took place in the middle of that cold Australian night in a yellow Holden car. The Creator of the universe poured out blessing into that car upon two very needy young men. He took a brand-new baby believer and through him lifted me out of the depth of my misery and despondency, never to doubt his reality again. And he took me, in my wretched state of personal need, and lifted a new but wavering child-in-the-faith, to nurture him and set his feet on the right path.

Does God Watch Football?

Nathan Brown

I was doing the tourist thing amid an unpleasant Victorian winter, and my experience of the southern climate was exacerbated by my recent descent from the warmer latitudes of Queensland. I was rapidly reaching the conclusion I was mad.

The cold was increased by the discomfort of intermittent showers. Nevertheless, foolishly, I'd decided to spend an evening on an 'eco-tour', discovering the nocturnal animals of the bush.

The group of adventurers gathered in the dark car park. Amid the preparations and delays, a woman at the back of the group let out a cry. The group turned toward her to observe the reason for her exclamation. We noticed a small radio held to her ear, which took all her attention. Seeing our glances, she smiled nervously, explaining, 'He got the ball.'

Her friends moved in. 'We had to drag her away from watching the football on TV,' they said. 'She's the mother of . . .' They gave a player's name and serial number, amazed at my ignorance of the Australian Football League.

But now, in light of her announcement, the anxious mother was treated with respect, particularly by a couple of the males.

We made our way into the dark, damp bush, pausing sporadically while the guide pointed out the occasional bedraggled and distant possum or some similar small furry creature. The murmur of radio static, fragments of football commentary and the muted cheers of the attentive listener punctuated these pauses, amid the dripping of cold rain and quiet of the bush.

As we trudged through the black night, I was struck by the commitment of this mother to her big, tough, football-playing son in another city, probably unaware of his mother's earnest attention to his every move via the radio commentary. That's a mother; that's football.

Umberto Eco says his first doubts about the existence of God and the meaning of life came to him as a teenager when he attended a soccer match. 'As I was observing with detachment the senseless movements down there on the field, I felt how the high noonday sun seemed to enfold men and things in a chilling light, and how before my eyes a cosmic, meaningless performance was proceeding,' he says.

Rather than imposing his own detached perspective, I wonder if Eco's conclusion may have been different if he had been observing the mother with whom I spent an evening wandering through the Victorian bush.

In the Bible, the question is asked as to whether a mother can forget her child or have no compassion toward that child. The answer is that even though that might happen—and, tragically, sometimes does—God will not forget you. God goes so far as to say, 'See, I have engraved you on the palms of my hands' (Isaiah 49:15–16).

So does God watch football? Of course he does. But it isn't from a lofty viewpoint, high in the grandstand. God watches football—and everything else you or I do in life—with the intensity of that mother, simultaneously cheering and fearing for us. He is saddened by our mistakes, excited by our successes and sympathetic to our hurts.

Even if a mother could forget her son, God would not forget us. He cares intensely, and he loves eternally.

Signposts

Ken Duncan

To the early American pioneers, the tower of Chimney Rock was a signpost of great significance—a spire of solitary grandeur rising more than 500 feet over the surrounding prairie. From far out on the plains, wagon-train outriders saw it as a guiding marker. The travellers' excitement grew as they drew near the rock, its presence reassuring them that they were on the Oregon Trail and that all was well on their trek to the western frontier lands. Boasting dependable spring waters, the area was ideal for camping, and in the shadow of the towering sentinel, the weary travellers took refuge from the gruelling track.

While photographing Chimney Rock in the tranquillity of this setting at sunrise, I felt as if I had been transported back in time to the early 1800s. I sensed the exhilaration of the early pioneers. The land has recorded their journey, and for those who will listen with their hearts, it now replays like a swirling, invisible mist.

I imagined the sounds of a campsite coming to life: campers rising with the sun and stoking fires to banish the chill of a desert night, with the whinny of a hobbled horse and the sound of twittering birds adding to the symphony. The early morning light hits the summit of the pinnacle first, giving it the appearance of a torch being held aloft. Slowly, then, the light works its way down the stunning formation to flood the prairie with its golden glow. A new day begins, and the travellers, now rejuvenated, are ready to continue their journey. Ahead lies the most difficult phase of all, the mountain passage. With all their worldly possessions bundled into wagons, they press onward, vulnerable on this epic adventure called life and humbled by the vast grandeur of the land.

The night after I had photographed Chimney Rock, I was restless and unable to shake the thoughts of that morning. I felt there was a lesson for me in the experience of those early settlers—a kind of parable about life in general. The pioneers had rejoiced at seeing Chimney Rock; it was a confirmation they were on the right track. But the rock was more than just a signpost. It also indicated a place where they could rest and be strengthened for the obstacles that lay ahead.

Life is a journey and can be fraught with difficulties. Along the way, many tracks lead from our path. The road seems long and the choices are many. What markers do we look for along the way to make sure we are on the right track and not just wandering around in the wilderness? Who is the trusted wagon master who guides our way and shows us the place of peace and rest?

Is it God in whom we trust?

The Devil Pushed Me

Fred Nile

My serious crisis of faith occurred in 1993. It filled me with doubt. I woke from a massive injection of painkillers in the Sydney Hospital next to the New South Wales Parliament House. My back screamed in pain and every breath was agonising.

X-rays had revealed three broken ribs only an inch (2.5 centimetres) from my spine. This was the result of a heavy fall six days previously on the steep stairs near the entrance of the Legislative Council at the rear of Parliament House. I had fallen backwards running down the stairs as the division bells rang for the critical vote on my Letona Cannery Financial Assistance Bill.

That one inch meant the difference between being a quadriplegic or even dying and just three broken ribs. When news of my injury became public, the *Daily Telegraph* ran a cartoon showing the devil pushing me down the stairs and God's angel catching me at the bottom. It was closer to the truth than the artist imagined.

As I lay in pain, like Job of the Old Testament I began to feel very sorry for myself. Outside my private room, loud shouts and screams floated up from Macquarie Street. Thousands of angry homosexual activists, unaware of my accident, were baying for my blood. 'We want Fred's head!' 'Better dead than Fred!' This was because I was leading the opposition to their 'victory' bill—the so-called 'Homosexual Vilification Bill'. This private member's bill had been introduced into the Lower House, the Legislative Assembly, by Clover Moore, the independent MP for Bligh (the homosexual ghetto). Ms Moore had boasted, 'My bill will gag Fred Nile.'

The bill would gag not only Fred Nile but all orthodox Christians and churches that took God's Word seriously. It would silence the historic Christian teaching critical of homosexuality, based on the Holy Bible.

This was my 'wilderness' experience, when the devil came to whisper in my ear, to tempt me as he tempted Jesus Christ in the wilderness. Because of my sorry physical state, the devil was able to get under my guard in a way he had never previously managed to achieve. As I lay alone in that darkened hospital room, with brown paper put across the windows by staff to hide my presence from the angry mob, the seeds of doubt started to grow into an irrational fear.

My whole life and witness had been confidently based on the Holy Bible, especially my uncompromising opposition to any legalising of homosexual acts or social acceptance of homosexuality. I thought I was doing God's work, obeying God's will. Yet could I be wrong and the mob screaming for my head be right? Had I misunderstood the Bible?

Had I been like a modern Pharisee throwing stones at the adulterous woman? Was it true I hated homosexuals? Did I really support 'gay bashing' because I opposed this bill—even though I had introduced at the same time the Crime Prevention Bill, which would have prohibited the incitement of violence against *any* person including homosexuals, but without putting them on a pedestal?

'Yes!' the devil shouted, 'Yes! You have been wrong all these years. Those clergy who have supported the homosexual movement, who have supported the ordination of homosexuals—they have been right. You have been wrong!'

I called out: 'Whose voice is this condemning me? Is it the Lord's or the devil's? Lord Jesus, help me to understand your will. Have I been wrong? Help me to honour the truth. If I've been wrong, O Lord, please forgive me!'

Then it seemed that with the eyes of faith—or was it a hallucination because of the painkillers?—I saw Jesus himself standing facing me at the foot of my hospital bed. With compassion in his eyes he began to speak, and the words came from his first recorded sermon, the Sermon on the Mount. In that sermon he warned his disciples of the coming days of persecution—persecution that would take the lives of the apostles and hundreds of thousands of other Christians from the time of the Emperor Nero right up to the present day.

Jesus lifted me up with his loving words, 'Blessed are those who are persecuted for righteousness' sake, for theirs is the kingdom of heaven.' I had certainly had my share of persecution because of my Christian convictions. 'Blessed are you when they revile you and persecute you, and say all kinds of evil against you falsely for my sake.' Well, I was being reviled on the streets of Sydney at that very moment, falsely accused of being a 'gay basher'. 'Rejoice and be exceedingly glad, for great is your reward in heaven, for so they persecuted the prophets who were before you.'

Then he reminded me that his followers are the salt of the earth and the light of the world. He said, 'Let your light so shine before men, that they may see your good works and glorify your Father in heaven.'

This clear word from the Lord was all the confirmation I needed. With all my human failings, I was carrying out God's will. My simple efforts to 'put myself in God's shoes', to see moral and social issues through God's eyes, had been correct. As we confronted complex moral issues, I prayed, 'Lord, help me to discern this issue, to see it through your eyes, to see it as a "black and white" issue, an issue of right or wrong.' It took a great deal of effort, but I had been successful.

Before this word from the Lord, I had resigned myself to being out of action, stuck in my hospital bed while the

Homosexual Vilification Bill went easily through the Upper House. Now the Lord renewed my faith, took away my doubts and replaced my weak 'wishbone' with a strong backbone. In spite of my three broken ribs, He said, 'Go back into the fight!'

About 8.00 p.m., my wife and fellow parliamentarian, Elaine, wheeled me in a wheelchair into the Upper House chamber with a great flurry of media activity. Like Cinderella I had to be back in hospital before midnight to have further painkillers.

As I am by nature a shy person, I never expected to be giving a speech in Parliament dressed in my pyjamas. In the following year's Mardi Gras, thirty homosexuals appeared in dressing gowns and riding in wheelchairs, wearing masks of my face! But this is a small price to pay for the privilege of being involved in the fight to maintain a society consistent with God's creative purposes for Planet Earth.

A Church with Sole

Michael Frost

The Subterranean Shoe Room is a very cool retro-shoe store in the hippest part of perpetually cool San Francisco. It was opened in Valencia Street a year or so ago by an unlikely proprietor.

Brock Bingaman is a Southern Baptist church planter/evangelist who came to San Francisco with every intention of planting a conventional purpose-driven type church. He had planted churches before, and one conversation with him reveals that he's an evangelist to his bootstraps.

But San Francisco is crawling with failed conventional purpose-driven type church planters. So secular, so culturally vigorous, so pro-gay is the city that the conventional church is withering on the vine. Crestfallen, young Brock realised that there was no point trying to re-create what many had tried and failed at before him. Needing gainful employment, Brock says he turned to his first love: shoes!

You see, Brock is the Imelda Marcos of the Southern

Baptist Convention. Ever since he was a boy he has collected shoes. He loves the darn things. When I told him I only own two or three pairs, he scoffed. 'I buy two or three pairs a week!' he laughed.

Together with his brother Josh and their wives, he rented a shop and filled it with new and retro (restored second-hand) shoes. Now he's doing a roaring trade in a fashion district that until the Subterranean Shoe Room opened only had a sports shoe outlet.

Brock has a special gift when it comes to shoes. He's no ordinary shoe salesman. He strikes up a conversation with those who browse his collection and when they tell him they're not sure what they're looking for, he has a standard retort. 'Tell me about yourself and I'll tell you what shoes you need.'

And so scores of San Franciscans have opened their lives up to him. After hearing their story, Brock tells them he has just the thing they're looking for and pulls out a pair of pink Pumas or cherry-red Docs. And he seems to get it right every time. It's like a scene from the movie *Chocolat*.

'As a church planter, I spent 90 per cent of my time with Christians,' he moans. 'Now, as a shoe salesman, I spend 90 per cent of my time with non-Christians.' He has developed significant relationships with gay couples, Marxist professors, aging hippies and bohemian artists. Just the kind of people you don't find in church. The walls of the Shoe Room are adorned with starving artists' work. He has sold a few pieces for them. His plan is to convert the basement at the Subterranean into a table tennis room (ping pong is back in San Francisco—go figure) and fill the place with local kids.

He hasn't led anyone to Jesus yet, but as an evangelist that is his heart's desire. It's a tough town to evangelise, and Brock has struck on a natural way to incarnate the message of the gospel to a people group normally hostile to Christianity. When he does start leading people to faith, he can't see that the church that blossoms out of the Subterranean will look like First Baptist Church down the road.

The Squatter and the Swaggie

Kel Richards

(Luke 16:19–23)

There was a wealthy squatter
Simply rolling in the dough.
All his ancestors before him
Had been wealthy so-and-so's.

He wore his moleskins and his boots,
As made by R. M. Williams;
He wore his coat of Harris Tweed
That made him look a million!

Though his sheep and cattle station
Was at least ten thousand acres,
He hated feeding swaggies,
Called them 'Lazy, lousy, fakers'.

Lying at his homestead gate
Was a sickly, older swaggie,
Who was looking pale and poorly
And quite positively daggy.

As he leaned against the gate post,
His swag all torn and tattered,
He said: 'I'm feeling awful crook,
And old, and tired, and battered.'

The swagman (name of Larry),
As he lay there thought: 'Perhaps
If the squatter has a banquet
Then, at least, I'll get the scraps.'

As the sickly swaggie lay there,
He spent his time in prayer.
But Sir William 'Wealthy Squatter'
Didn't pray—he didn't care.

The station dogs came sniffing round,
The swaggie counted seven,
And then he fell asleep—and woke
To find himself—in heaven!

Meanwhile, the wealthy squatter
Ate his foods all fat and fried
Until his arteries closed up,
And the squatter also died.

The squatter had a funeral
That was positively flash.
The VIPs all came along
To show respect for all that cash!

But the squatter found himself
In Outer Darkness ... feeling needy.
'I hate this place,' he sadly said,
'It's hot as Coober Pedy!'

And then he glimpsed the swaggie,
In a place that looked real nice.
'Oy!' yelled out the squatter,
'You there! In paradise!

'I'm here frying in the darkness
While I guess you've got it made.
Can't you send me down a little help?
Say, a nice cool lemonade?'

'There's a chasm fixed between us,'
Were the words of the reply.
'You should have prayed before you died,
Now's too late, don't even try.'

'Please listen,' said the squatter,
'To one last request I'll make:
Could Larry Swaggie please go back
And warn my folks, for goodness' sake?

'I have, you see, five brothers—
At the homestead they are gathered.
They musn't end up where I am,
That's what really matters.'

The reply that came from heaven
Said: 'Your brothers have the Bible.
That's the book in which God speaks,
It's both truthful and reliable.'

'No! No!' called out the squatter
From his place of dark despair,
'They'll all ignore the Bible,
They won't think to find truth there.

'But if someone from the dead comes back
Then they'll know the score.'
The sad reply from heaven said:
'They won't listen any more.

'Their hearts are hard, their minds are fixed,
On selfish insurrection;
And they ignore the evidence
Of historic resurrection.'

Radio Saved Her Life

Gordon Moyes

Many remarkable stories have come out of my years doing four hours every Sunday night on the number one radio station in Australia, 2GB. One story concerns a call that came in one night at about five minutes to midnight. The caller was a sobbing young woman. Her name was Melody.

Later Melody wrote a full account of what happened. Here it is in her own words:

> It was the winter of 1988, cold and pouring with rain. After 11.30 p.m. I was driving back to Sydney, having spent the weekend in Canberra saying goodbye to friends. I had decided that the only way out of my problems was to kill myself.
>
> I had no self-esteem, believing that the abuse I suffered as a child and a young teenager was all my fault. As the trucks came thundering towards me out of the dark,

I thought how easy it would be to steer my car underneath the front of one of them. It would be a quick and easy death.

As I drove I usually listened to cassettes, but on this particular night I turned on the radio to see if I could find a friendly voice. As I listened I heard the announcer say that if anyone wanted him to pray for them, then to give him a call. It was Gordon Moyes on 2GB, and immediately I knew I had to call. *I have to stop and phone*, I thought. *This is my only chance.*

I was just leaving Goulburn, and as I looked to the side of the road, there was a phone booth. I rattled in my purse for change, wondering if it would work. It did, and I was put straight through to Gordon on air. I was pretty upset and it took a while for me to tell him why I had called. But I remember he just kept talking to me. He didn't even say the prayer he normally says when he closes the program.

After the show finished, he kept talking to me off air. That telephone and that link with another human being became my only hold on life. When we eventually stopped talking, I had calmed down a little and begun to see that maybe there was some way out of the deep depression I had sunk into. Gordon made me promise to call him as soon as I got home. I remember the relief in his voice when I called him at 2:30 that morning to say I had arrived home safely. When we were talking on air, he had asked people to pray for me. Those prayers were the only thing that carried me through that night and beyond.

During my teenage years I had always blamed myself for everything that had ever gone wrong. I felt utterly worthless. My life had no purpose, and all I could see was that I had caused problems for everyone. In my depression I decided that the best thing I could do was to kill myself so I wouldn't be a burden anymore.

That late night call to Gordon on 2GB turned my life around—a complete about-face. I began to see that what had happened to me was not my fault. I was not responsible for what others had done to me. After I understood that and put the blame squarely on those who had done wrong, I was able to take the next step in the process of healing—to forgive those who had hurt me.

I had also made the decision to take God at his word and believe that what the Bible said was absolutely true. If God said he loved me in his Word, then God loved me! I also read the story of the unforgiving servant in Matthew 18:23–35. God had forgiven me many things, and I started to see that God also loved those who had hurt me and had sent Jesus to die for them as well. Slowly it sank into my heart: if God could love and forgive them, who was I to hold something against them? My only option was to forgive them and trust God with their lives.

That step brought such freedom into my heart. For the first time I really saw what Jesus meant when he said, 'I came that they might have life, and have it abundantly' (John 10:10, NASB).

Since that time my life has been filled with God's love and the joy of sharing his gospel of redemption, grace and wholeness with others. The change in me wasn't something that happened instantly—it was a process that had to be diligently worked through. It couldn't have been done without the love and support of friends who let me cry and who prayed for me.

Because of all that God had done in my life, I wanted to work full-time for him. The opportunity arose for me to go to Africa at the beginning of 1990. It was a fantastic time of seeing God's faithfulness over and over again as he supplied my every need and taught me constantly from his Word. My own spiritual life grew amazingly, and it was such a joy to see people change radically on hearing of the grace of God and the salvation he has made ours in Jesus.

I spent seven months in South Africa, a month in Zimbabwe and England, and three months in Canada. Each place was different, and in each place God had different things he wanted to emphasise to me. But in them all, God's Word was 'I love you'. This is what has given me the strength to go on when my life seemed worthless.

Now I'm back in Australia and grateful for the opportunity to say thank you to anyone who heard that first call to 2GB and who prayed for me. And to those of you who have friends who are struggling with thoughts of suicide and worthlessness, don't give up hope. In Jeremiah 29:11, God declares: 'I know the plans I have for you, plans for welfare and not for calamity, to give you a future and a hope' (NASB).

I well remember the night a tearful Melody rang me at five minutes to midnight in the pouring rain from a phone box outside Goulburn. As she sobbed out her story, I said to my listeners, 'Now, I always close with my prayer, but tonight I don't want to have this prayer because I want to keep talking to Melody. Those of you who are Christians, would you please pray for me and Melody while we have this discussion, and I'm quite sure your prayers will help us resolve this problem.'

So the program ended without the prayer as usual. But out among my listeners, many people earnestly prayed for Melody and for my discussion.

Over the next half hour or so, I talked to Melody on the phone. I suggested that she continue on towards Sydney and I would drive out to Liverpool to meet her. However, she eventually said she felt confident to drive home to Lane Cove and ring me from there, which she did. I made arrangements to meet her the next day. Then over the next few weeks we met several times, and one of my staff provided Melody with a great deal of encouragement and help.

Her life was put back into order, and her visit to Africa, which she mentioned, was an absolute triumph for her as she went to help some of the most underprivileged and poor people in the world.

From time to time I still talk with Melody, and whenever I do I feel deeply grateful to God for the people who prayed during our discussion that night over a decade ago. Some time after it happened, an elderly lady wrote to me and told me she had heard Melody's suicide call. She explained that when she heard me say I was going to keep talking to Melody and asked listeners to pray, 'I got out of bed and knelt beside my bed and prayed for Melody as if she were my own granddaughter. I prayed over and over again; in fact, it was daylight before I got up from my knees.'

God heard her prayers, and as a result Melody is living a fruitful and effective life today. Who knows just what the outcome of our sincere and effective prayers will be?

Living for Tomorrow

Amanda Smith

We left Australia in 1989, dewy-eyed newly-weds. We enjoyed the adventure of the student life: the furniture that comes in a box, the tiny flats, the hand-me-down car. But we were always waiting for life to really begin, for a degree to be finished, to settle down, to move back home to Australia.

But things did not go as planned. A door shut and another opened and we found ourselves in America again. So there we were, nine years later, still in America. Somehow we got the 'real' furniture, the 'real' job, the 'real' post-student life. But we were still not home. Life can't really start until we're home!

But then a baby arrived . . . and another. If only we could get back home! 'Yes, she was born in America but she's really an Australian.' 'No, he's never been to Australia, but I'm sure he'll have an Aussie accent.'

And yet, these children's lives continue, changing and growing everyday. As much as I long to, I cannot put them on hold until they are with their cousins and grandparents, until they can awaken to the raucous cacophony of kookaburras. They may one day be teenagers in Australia, but they will never be babies there, to experience their early years again in that familiar place of my childhood. They are Americans. They have Australian parents, yes, but they are Americans. It's their home; it's all they've ever known.

And suddenly I see I've been living my entire life on hold: hesitating to deepen a friendship in case I leave, refusing to buy any electrical appliances because they won't work with the Australian current, even putting up with a pillow like a pancake because we may go home soon and I'll just buy a new one there.

Don't we all do this in some way or another? Don't we all miss some idealised past or put our present on hold for some ideal future?

'Life will be great when I have kids.'

'Life will be great when the kids grow up and move out.'

'Life will be great when I get the perfect job.'

'Life will be great when I retire.'

'Life will be great when I can finally buy a home.'

'Life will be great when I can finally finish these house repairs.'

Why do we cherish the past sentimentally and long for the future with anticipation, but have no regard for the present? After all, today is just yesterday's future and tomorrow's past.

What do I have today that I once longed for or that I will someday miss? How can I enjoy it now while I have it?

As the writer of Ecclesiastes says: 'Do not say, "Why is it that the former days were better then these?" For it is not from wisdom that you ask about this . . . If a man should live many years, let him rejoice in them all' (7:10, 11:8, NASB).

So here I am, still living in America, still regretting that my kids aren't growing up in the place of my childhood. But now I'm investing in relationships and putting down roots here. I even went out and got myself that new pillow!

And as much as I would like to live back in Australia, and as beautiful as Australia is, life there will not be perfect, and one day I will miss some things from this strange place. I know that, regardless of where I am, one day I will long to read just one more story to my three-year-old daughter or giggle once more with my five-month-old son.

So no more 'Life *will be* great when . . .' Life *is* great! Here. Today. Now.

God's Improbable Choices

John Mallison

The Bible is filled with stories of the most unexpected people whom God chose, transformed and empowered to do outstanding things for him. Moses, the liberator and leader of a nation, apparently had a speech impediment. David was the youngest in a large family and only a lowly shepherd boy when he was chosen and anointed as the future king.

Jeremiah, the Old Testament prophet, was certainly one of God's surprises. Sensitive, reticent and introspective, he had a deep sense of personal inadequacy and lived a lonely existence. Yet God called and empowered this unlikely person to warn of his impending judgment. This he did faithfully and with amazing courage for forty years, with no apparent positive response from most of his hearers.

For much of my childhood and teenage years I was a very shy person. When I was a small child, my older sister often said, as I hid behind her in the presence of strangers, 'He doesn't speak; I speak for him!'

Well into my teens, I shunned any situation where I had to face a large group that was unknown to me.

However, after I committed my life to Jesus Christ at the age of sixteen, there was a marked change in my self-confidence. At nineteen I was preaching without any sense of nervousness. Indeed, the minister of my church, who had a hunch about my gifts and gave me that first opportunity to preach, was quite overwhelmed by the assurance of my manner and the impact on the congregation. Since that time, I have conducted training events with up to 1500 involved, and preached to as many as 11,000 without once feeling apprehensive.

Although I have always been creative with my hands and did very well at high school in technical subjects, English was my 'weakest link'. Now many books dealing with the practical aspects of Christian ministry bear my name, with some becoming best-sellers and even being translated into other languages.

My life and work is a testimony to what God can do with a most unlikely person. Occasionally my wife has lovingly said to me, 'You are an ordinary person to whom God has given extraordinary opportunities'—with which I heartily agree!

Jesus chose a most improbable group to be his initial disciples. Mark, in his gospel, depicts them in a surprisingly unfavourable light. In Jesus' band there were seemingly irreconcilable elements and a great variety of temperaments and dispositions. His followers were of modest means and limited schooling, virtually unknown to all but those in their immediate community. Yet Jesus took an incredible risk with these people. To them he confidently committed the future of his message and mission, after they had been mentored by him for a comparatively short period. Jesus helps us understand that God can use anyone and often the most unlikely.

I have worked closely with some of the world's best-known Christian leaders. All have been extremely competent in their specific fields of ministry. But frequently I have found on closer acquaintance that those who have impressed me most have been very modest and unassuming.

Their whole attitude and demeanour has reflected the Apostle Paul's testimony: 'I am what I am by the grace of God.'

Someone has said, 'Moses spent forty years as a prince in Pharaoh's court, thinking he was somebody. He spent forty years as a hired hand in a harsh desert, learning he was nobody. He then spent forty years leading the children of Israel, discovering what God can do with a person who has realised they are a nobody without him.'

God has to keep teaching me the painful lesson that I am not essentially an outstanding person, a prince in Pharaoh's court, but an 'improbable choice'—someone whom God, in his love and grace, chooses to use, often in quite unexpected ways.

A Small Butterfly

Margaret Reeson

The butterfly is small and beautiful. It was hand-carved with love out of a fragment of timber from a family home that was destroyed in a bushfire. The wood carver, John, asked his friends for permission to search in the ruins of their home at Helensburg, New South Wales, for any timber that may have survived the inferno. He found only a short length of wood that had not been reduced to charcoal, but from this he carved four butterflies.

On the back of the wings he polished the wood to retain the black charring—a reminder that the butterflies came from a time of terrible loss.

One of the four butterflies was given to me. At the time of the fires (Christmas 2001–New Year 2002), I was serving in the role of Moderator of the New South Wales Synod of the Uniting Church in Australia, and in that role I was able to visit a number of the areas that had been affected. The butterfly went with me. It was a profoundly moving experience.

The fires had been extinguished by the time I travelled to the regions that had been burned—west of Sydney around Mulgoa, Silverdale and Warragamba; in the Blue Mountains at Warrimoo; south of the city in the communities of Helensburg and Heathcote; and further south in the Illawarra along the Princes Highway and in the communities of Sussex Inlet and St Georges Basin.

But although the fires were out, the wounds were raw. Bush was blackened. Large areas of national park appeared to have been destroyed. Timber telegraph poles and fence posts were charred and in danger of collapse. Heavy metal road signs at major intersections had been warped by the intense heat and lettering had melted away. Burnt out vehicles stood beside the ruins of houses.

The random fury of the flames had taken some homes, businesses, orchards and livestock, and left others standing. A householder made a collection of black objects to symbolise the intensity of the fire through his property, including a metal bar which was all that was left of a melted wheelie bin. A church congregation shared a Christmas cake for morning tea in February: 'We all missed Christmas,' they said.

And yet there were so many signs of courage and hope. Many images stay with me.

The courage of firefighters is the stuff of legend. One experienced volunteer firefighter described driving toward the oncoming fire with his son as they attempted to reach homes that might be saved. Headlights of retreating vehicles coming towards them were barely visible through the thick smoke, but they went on. Their radio informed them that their own street was being evacuated in another part of the community. A falling branch and burning bark landed on their vehicle. 'It put the wind up us,' he said. But they, and countless others, were part of saving lives and property.

Another volunteer firefighter described working for ten to eighteen hours every day for two weeks during the crisis. It is not surprising that we saw many hand-painted signs outside surviving houses, often standing within a burnt area, with messages like 'God bless the firefighters' and 'Fireys are angels. Thanks.'

Practical acts of kindness took many forms—in emergency hospitality, meals and beds, communication with relatives, chaplaincy and reassurance in anxiety. Elderly residents of a retirement village were touched by the care taken of them when they were evacuated in the middle of the night. Neighbours in a suburban street defended the home of friends who had gone away for Christmas. Some people in need were handed an anonymous envelope from a local Christian community and found in it a valuable gift of emergency cash. Over and over, it was clear that many people were assuming that everyone else's need was greater than their own.

On the day I visited one badly damaged suburban street, demolition teams were working to remove the remains of burnt-out houses. Two women who were residents in that street made a request for help from our church for their neighbours. 'Not for the people who have lost everything,' they explained, 'because they are already getting substantial help. We want to give something—maybe a weekend away from the smell of burning—to those who have been very frightened and have lost some things but won't be getting any compensation.' Later, a letter arrived from the minister of a different church in that area. He pointed out that the women who had made the request had suffered as much loss as their neighbours, but had asked for nothing for themselves.

Signs of hope were everywhere. Brilliant new red-orange leaves were bursting from the charcoal bark of eucalypts, forcing their way out from trees that seemed dead. From the ash on the floor of bushland in national parks, ferns were uncurling. Tall black tree trunks wore an exuberant overcoat of green leaves. Rebuilding of homes and businesses had begun. A woman had parked a caravan near the ashes of her home, her farm shed, the remnants of unburned garden and the twisted remains of her car. 'I'm staying here and starting again,' she said.

In one rural area, where several church families had lost property and been through a very disturbing experience, they told their stories to me over a meal. One couple said, 'The worst moment of all was driving back up the road towards our property after being evacuated for three days. We had no idea if we would find anything left, and no one could tell us.' Miraculously, their house had survived, but much of their business was gone.

I showed them the little wooden butterfly, which I was wearing as a brooch, and told them about that other Uniting Church congregation. 'The family who lost their home lost everything,' I told them. 'Trophies, university work, handmade quilts . . .' A few weeks later I learned that the country congregation had decided that, as they had several quilters among them, they would like to make a banner for their church to express their faith in the love of God and the reality of new life, despite the destruction of bushfire—and would make something to send to that other family and their Christian community.

The little wooden butterfly has visited many places now and brought its own message of hope. It is a gift from God to us all. It is a sign of hope, a sign of restoration and a future, of renewed life. It is also a sign that we belong together. The fears and tears of part of our family touch us all. The hurt and anxiety of our brothers and sisters give us pain. And we can be part of the healing and hope for each other.

The wood carver told me that he usually carves in specially selected and beautiful timbers. 'This one is only a bit of pine, nothing special.' I don't agree. This fragment of wood is very precious indeed.

The Unseen Hand

Dudley Foord

Recently I was in Broome, a city in north-west Australia famous for its pearling industry. While there I was able to gain some understanding of the dangerous pearl-shell industry. Australian pearls are reputed to be the best in the world and are much sought after because of their unique and attractive qualities.

The deep sea diver must wear a special suit as he works on the sea bed many metres below the surface. Special pipes carrying oxygen and other vital necessities for life are provided by the service ship above. The diver works in a hostile environment. If a pipe is cut or fails he cannot survive. The dangers are considerable.

There are some parallels between the diver's life and life for a Christian in a secular world that seems to have no place for the living God. The Bible is clear that the Christian lives in a hostile environment. Jesus said to his disciples, 'I send you out as lambs among wolves.' In the famous and much loved passage in John 15, nine times he uses the words 'hatred and persecution' to describe the milieu of the world of the Christian's existence. He also brings marvellous warmth and encouragement to the Christian in his memorable words, 'I am the vine; you are the branches.'

Here he is helping us to grasp the special relationship that exists between the Christian and Christ. In this connected relationship of the vine and the branch, the branch is sustained by the life-giving sap of the vine. Christians can, therefore, live joyful, positive and meaningful lives in a hostile environment because of this 'invisible' relationship with the Lord of the whole universe.

Having found the pearl of great price, Christians delight to walk with God on their journey through the labyrinth of this confusing and chaotic world to heaven. They are sustained by their 'unseen' relationship with the risen and reigning Christ.

Bible quotations are from Luke 10:3, NKJV; John 15:5.

It's Raining Men

Darlene Zschech

Here's a great little story for you about my girlfriend.

When she was only very young, and had been a Christian for just a few weeks, she asked her youth leader if she and a group of her newly-saved friends could do a dance item in church. The youth leader was really keen to encourage these beautiful new converts, and so without seeing or listening to what they were about to do, he said, 'Cool! Come dance for us all.'

Well, the blood ran from his face as these innocent but extremely enthusiastic girls started dancing to 'It's Raining Men' by The Weather Girls. The chorus says, 'It's raining men, Hallelujah!' and so the girls thought it was a godly song! Oops!

The church was mortified. And yet somehow I can see all of heaven smiling and cheering as the new babes in Christ brought their offering.

The Not-Sure Syndrome

Kim Hawtrey

At last the big day had arrived. The guests were seated in the church and the groom, whose name was Bill, was standing at the front of the assembly dressed in his new suit. Beside him stood the best man. Any moment now the bride would arrive.

All of a sudden, there she was. Resplendent in her finery, with father on her arm ready to give her away, Vicki began the procession down the aisle. She was followed by the bridesmaids. The whole scene looked a picture as Vicki took her place alongside Bill and the packed church looked on.

The marriage service began. Everything proceeded normally until they came to the part about making promises.

The minister addressed Bill with the standard question he had asked a thousand times before of other grooms: 'Do you take this woman to be your lawful wedded wife?'

Bill appeared surprised. He seemed stunned by the question, like a rabbit caught in a car's headlights.

'Could . . . could you . . . repeat the question, please?' Bill stammered.

A giggle went through the congregation. Just a case of a young man with nerves, everybody thought.

The minister chuckled to himself and, with an amused smile, asked again: 'Bill, do you take Vicki to be your lawful wedded wife?'

'Why, I'm not sure,' Bill replied. A hushed murmur went through the crowd. 'What I mean is, I'd prefer to keep an open mind on the matter.'

A few people shifted uncomfortably in their seats.

'Don't get me wrong,' Bill continued 'I'm not saying I don't believe in Vicki. I do believe—in my own way. It's just that, well, my beliefs are a private matter and I feel they should stay that way.'

You could have cut the air with a knife. Vicki was looking aghast at Bill. The congregation was by now extremely agitated. The bride's mother was on the point of fainting, and the bride's father was on the verge of picking a fight—with the groom.

The minister thought he would try one final time: 'William Jones,' he boomed, staring straight at the hapless Bill, 'will you or will you not take Victoria to be your lawful wedded wife?'

Bill seemed stuck for an answer. By now the place was in an uproar and it was all too much for Vicki. She turned and stormed back down the aisle, taking the bridesmaids with her. The best man put the ring back into his pocket. The guests began to file out of the church, and within minutes the place was empty except for Bill, who was left standing by himself, wondering what all the fuss was about.

'What was it I said?' he asked himself. 'After all, it wasn't as if I said no!'

This is not a true story. But I tell it to make a point: there are certain situations in life where not saying yes is equivalent to saying no. One of those situations is your wedding day. Another is your response to God and his gospel.

There is a widespread spiritual syndrome today of 'not-surism'. While most folk may not espouse outright atheism, many try to get away with the more subtle approach of not-surism. This means stopping short of saying no to Jesus while at the same time never saying yes to him. Perhaps they say something like 'I believe in my own way' or 'I think there are many valid ways to God'.

This simply will not do. It is behaving exactly like Bill on his wedding day. The basic problem lies in trying to 'keep an open mind' about a matter that requires a yes or no answer.

I'm sure you will agree with me when I say that Vicki had every right to interpret Bill's response as a no. In the same way, Jesus is entirely justified in reading our not-sure attitude towards him as a rejection.

The Heart of O'Doherty

Irene Voysey

Stephen O'Doherty once thought the Bible was anachronistic and self-contradictory. Love and the prayers of a young woman changed his mind.

Georgina and Stephen fell in love late in 1986, but she was a Christian and decided their friendship would have to remain strictly platonic. Even the pressures of his career in broadcast journalism were nothing compared to the range of emotions that buffeted Stephen. He was devastated, but also clinically curious.

Here was a lovely girl who was very intelligent (she was on her way to a PhD in biology) yet prepared to hold firm to a faith which he had always thought belonged to the weak and gullible. 'You could even say I persecuted Christians,' Stephen admits. Now the very foundations of his life, based on his decision at the age of fifteen to be an atheist, were being soundly shaken.

Georgina was also torn emotionally. She desperately loved

Stephen, yet she was determined to obey the Word of God and its sensible teaching not to marry someone whose life had an entirely different focus to her own. Their discussions late into the night on the meaning of Christianity only strengthened her resolve.

Valentine's Day 1987 saw a nervous Georgina giving Stephen an unusual Valentine's Day gift—a pocket-sized New Testament. 'I was worried that I might have been pushing too far and putting him off the idea of considering the Christian faith,' she says. Stephen's response was a great relief to her. 'I've been wanting to get hold of a Bible for some time,' he said. Her inscription in the front cover was, he says, 'Spot on'. Georgina had written, 'May you find the happiness and peace you are seeking—I hope this book helps'.

With a journalist's critical eye Stephen began at the beginning, reading and mentally processing the information as if it were a government report. The genealogy of Jesus in Matthew chapter one did not impress him. 'Then, as I read on, that little book came alive and began to speak to me directly,' he says. 'By the time I reached the Sermon on the Mount I was really shaken. Everything I'd believed for the past twelve years was severely threatened.'

Slowly and quietly over the next few months he considered the gospel and his response to it, reading the Bible, talking to Christians and attending church with Georgina. One day he was drawn to take communion at the Lord's table, and the Holy Spirit at last filled Stephen's heart and life.

And what about that 'self-contradictory book', the Bible? Stephen's response is the succinct summary of a seasoned journalist, one who had been the state political correspondent for the *7:30 Report* in 1989, the national affairs reporter for the *Walsh Report* in 1990 and the host of 2GB's Breakfast Show in 1991, when the program was attracting a listening audience of well over 300,000 people each week. 'The Bible is a truly remarkable series of books that tell a totally consistent story which spans centuries,' he says firmly.

Stephen and Georgina were married in September 1988.

'Image builders in the communications industry promote and advertise and build up a media personality, and if you're not careful you finish up believing all the things they say about you,' Stephen says. 'Then if the ratings drop and your program is axed, suddenly no one wants to know you. It's as if you never existed. My security and strength come from being a child of God, working wherever he wants me to serve, and learning more about him daily.'

Stephen moved from radio broadcasting into New South Wales state politics in 1991, eventually becoming Shadow Minister for Education and Training and finally Shadow Treasurer. Despite the temptations of the world of politics and power, an extension of what Stephen sees as 'The Image Industry', his faith in Jesus Christ survived.

In 2002 he began to serve God in yet another new role, this time as the Chief Executive Officer of Christian Schools Australia, a coalition of Christian schools. Stephen says, 'Christian education is an area in which I will continue serving the wider community, supporting the development of schools and contributing to the debate about values and character, excellence and choice in education.'

And where does his wisdom come from as he considers values, character and excellence for today's generation? Naturally, it is based on the Bible, the book Stephen O'Doherty once believed was anachronistic.

Never, Never Give Up

Dudley Foord

I was sitting in a doctor's waiting room one day when I picked up a magazine and read a curious little story. It came from an Australian farming community.

Three frogs, it seemed, fell into a container of rich, creamy milk. They swam around looking for a way out but found none. Soon one frog gave up hope and sank to the bottom and drowned. The remaining two persevered at swimming around, hoping that some way out would be discovered. After some time the second frog lost hope, sank and drowned.

The last frog was determined to solve his dilemma by continuing to swim and paddle around. Soon he felt something solid. Hope rekindled, he continued to paddle and swim, paddle and swim, until gradually the liquid became more and more solid and he was able to jump out free. All his paddling had turned the milk into cream and the cream into butter.

The punch line of the story was: 'Never, never give up.'

Sir Winston Churchill was once invited to speak to the boys from his childhood school. On the appointed day, all the boys were prepared with paper and pens ready to jot down his famous Churchillian statements. But they were deeply disappointed when all Churchill said was, 'Young gentlemen, never give up. Never, ever, ever give up.' Then he sat down.

Disappointed, yes. But those boys never forgot what he said and were deeply influenced to develop persevering characters.

One greater than Churchill, the Lord of the universe, said: 'He who endures [perseveres] to the end will be saved' (Matthew 10:22, NKJV). God's promises and commands are always accompanied by his enablings to do what is commanded.

Never give up!

Answers to Prayer

Brian Pickering

There had been no previous indications of a developing problem, so when I tried to rise up from bending over weeding the garden and felt my back go on me, I thought a little rest would be all I would need to get myself back into shipshape form.

A few days' bed rest and no improvement resulted in a trip to the doctor, but again complete rest was the only suggested cure. Another week went by and I noted some improvement, so I resumed work although the pain had by no means disappeared.

As there were good days and bad days and the pain was persisting, the doctor ordered physiotherapy to help my recovery. This treatment had some success. But then after a few days of reduced pain my back would 'go' on me again and I would be back to where I was the week before. The doctor became more concerned as nothing he tried seemed to provide any long-term relief. He referred me to a specialist.

Initially the specialist also believed that proper rest combined with physiotherapy would bring the relief I sought. A brace was specially manufactured for me to wear during the day to support my back and ease the pain. It was somewhat bulky and awkward to wear, so at night I tried to get by without it. However, many times I had to lie on the floor to eat or to obtain some kind of relief from the pain.

All of this time many people were praying for my healing. At every opportunity I was prayed for at meetings, church services or by concerned friends. I believed within myself that God healed, but as time went on without an apparent answer, doubts began to arise within me as to whether he was going to heal *me*. A crisis of faith was looming on the horizon.

As days turned into weeks, the specialist became more vexed at my lack of progress. X-rays were taken along with other tests and finally the crushing diagnosis was delivered. My condition was one of the premature ageing of the spinal discs in my back. In other words, the normal ageing process that begins in later life was happening in my body in my early twenties.

I was told that my future was bleak. I would need to learn to live with the pain or undergo surgery that had only a 50/50 chance of success. The surgical option involved fusing my spine. If successful, this would result in some loss of movement in my body. If unsuccessful, it would leave me in a wheelchair for the rest of my life.

At this time my wife and I were about to have our first child. I felt totally helpless. I did not want my wife to have to give up her life to care for an invalid husband. I did not want my children to miss out on being able to have all the pleasure that an active father can give them. Suddenly I had to face a huge decision. Could I trust God to heal me, or should I allow medical science to try its best without guarantee of success? I put off the day of the decision for six months to give God time to respond to my prayers for help.

I attended every healing service I could find. I had every person I knew praying for me. I cried out to God myself. All to no avail. My faith was beginning to fade. People began making excuses as to why I wasn't being healed. I began to resign myself to a life of pain and limited movement.

Then one morning, as I stood alone in the kitchen of our home, I had an encounter with God. He spoke to me. 'Brian, I have not left you, but I have been waiting for you to come to the end of yourself, to give up looking for your healing in every direction and to look only to me.' I heard him ask the question, 'Do you want to be healed?'

'Of course I do,' I said. 'You know I've been crying out for you to heal me for months.'

'Then reach out and take my hand and you will be healed.'

In that moment, a supernatural portion of faith was gifted to me by God. In the Spirit, I reached out and took his hand and received his gift of healing. That was more than thirty years ago, so I have had many years of proving that the healing was indeed miraculous and permanent. God met me not just in my need but in my desperation, and reminded me that he had never left me.

Yes, God answers prayer, but not always the first time we ask, and often not in the way or with the timing we expect. He often lets us try everything and everyone else, and only when we have exhausted all other avenues does he come with the reminder, 'I have never left you—do you want me to help you?'

The Gates of Hell

Geoff Bullock

The trip from the Golan Heights to Caesarea Philippi was steep. The narrow road descended, winding around barren hills, levelling out through small towns. We travelled for an hour or so until at the bottom of the last hill we turned into what was obviously another tourist spot.

As always our guide shouted instructions. We were to gather in a small garden beside a stream where I, as the tour leader, would attempt to inspire our travel-weary friends. I grabbed my Bible and stayed behind with the guide.

'Where are we?' I asked him.

His answer stopped me in my tracks.

'We are at the ruins of an ancient pagan temple that was built into the hillside surrounding a huge cave. A subterranean river runs through this cave, emerging at the garden where we are about to meet. This temple was a centre for pagan worship. Thousands of innocent children and young virgin girls were sacrificed here to appease the gods.

According to accepted tradition, this is where Jesus asked his disciples, "Who do you say that I am?" It is called "the Gates of Hell".'

Can you see what I saw?

Jesus brought his disciples to this accursed place. As Jews, they were standing on unclean soil. Perhaps they looked around and secretly hoped that no one would see them.

Jesus pointed to the ruins, ruins that spoke volumes about who humanity thought God to be. These ruins were a worship manual concerning what the god of this temple required from the worshipper who sought blessing and favour. The temple would have run red with the blood of those who were sacrificed according to the laws and precepts of their bloodthirsty, vengeful god.

These ruins were humanity's response to the question that God the Father had asked through Jesus: 'Who do you say that I am?'

At the heart of this temple worship was the mistaken requirement that God would 'do this' if the worshipper 'did that'. What the worshipper did varied from small, simple favours that God blessed to horrid murderous sacrifices, but the intent and expectation remained the same. This was a God who required our actions *before* he performed his.

This is a common perception of God. It has its extreme in this temple site, but its philosophy stretches throughout time to all who seek to be blessed according to their actions. This temple, and all the 'temples' that have followed, say to the worshipper: 'Give more, pray harder, bring a greater sacrifice. If God is not answering your prayers, then you must work, work, work at your "worship".'

What is this 'worship'? It is anything from the horrid hell of child sacrifice to the simple acts that ask God to respond. When we 'worship' this way, we are forever locked into performances that have to be increasingly pure, increasingly disciplined and increasingly presented. God's favour is presumed to be conditional, and we are locked into fear of doing anything that would cause his rejection. We fall into the trap of examining everything we do just in case we are not measuring up. We pray, study, give, work and exhaust ourselves because we are afraid to stop. We are afraid of rejection. We are scared of God.

Jesus came to this temple, the tragic exaggeration of this 'blessings and cursings formula', and simply asked, 'Is this necessary?'

If the disciples had seen who he really was, then they had seen for themselves what God requires of his worshippers. It certainly isn't this temple. Could they see that the truth must extend beyond this temple to the fundamental principles of humanity's need of acceptance?

Peter's answer sealed the truth. Every pagan temple, every guilt-stricken worshipper, every work and sacrifice, was now rendered obsolete and unnecessary.

'You are the Christ, the Son of the living God.'

You are the embodiment of all that God is, does and requires.

Jesus stood outside this temple dedicated to the 'if you do this, I will do that' doctrine and affirmed Peter's revelation:

> 'Blessed are you, Simon Bar-Jonah, for flesh and blood has not revealed this to you, but my Father who is in heaven. And I also say to you that you are Peter, and on this rock I will build My church, and the gates of Hades [hell] shall not prevail against it.'

Suddenly, as I stood in the car park surrounded by tourist buses, I saw the most wonderful truth. As the disciples looked up at the huge rock looming above them, with its ruins and its cave of sacrifice, Jesus was saying to them:

'The rock on which I will build my kingdom is not the rock of your sacrifices, works and deeds. It is the rock of who the Messiah is, what he does and what he requires. It is not about what you do; it is about what I will do. When that is understood, then this place and all the other conditional "gates of hell" will never again torment worshippers with the guilt and insufficiency of what they do and cannot do.'

I looked up at the ruins of this temple and realised that the 'gates of hell' only admitted those who came carrying their own sacrifices. These were cruel gates that demanded worship, sacrifice, standards and fear. These gates fall when Jesus' church opens its doors to admit all who come—those on the 'inside' as well as those 'outside'. All the flawed and failed sons and daughters of the kingdom. We all come with this free ticket—a ticket that we can never afford. A ticket that is bought by grace and received by faith.

Bible quotations are from Matthew 16, NKJV.

Grace-Filled Living

Michael Frost

I know of a church in a new housing area of Sydney that was trying to hold two Sunday services each week and getting very little interest in the evening service. The morning worship meeting drew a good number, but at night only six to ten people turned up. Sensing that it was silly to duplicate their limited resources, they decided to close the evening service.

This isn't an unusual story. Many small or new congregations have only a Sunday morning service.

But the manner in which they closed the service was unique. They invited the dozen or so people who were attending the service to covenant to use the time they would normally be in church to do something special for the community instead.

Some people committed themselves to serve in the local soup kitchen. Another volunteered to take calls at a child sponsorship program. One couple decided to spend the hour they normally sat in church on Sunday evening pushing their newborn child in a baby carriage around their neighbourhood. Of course, everyone stops young parents in the street to coo at a new baby. As people watered their lawns or washed their cars, they started up conversations with the Christian couple. This couple told me they had made more friendships, shared the love of Jesus more often and generally been more effective as salt and light in their community since they stopped going to church and started pushing a baby carriage.

Many churches close services and their members are free to take a Sunday evening stroll. But by inviting people to see their substitute activity as *mission*, this church saw a whole raft of new possibilities emerging.

Our socialising must be intentional, missional, grace-filled and generous. It must be seen as part of a broader pattern of showing compassion within a community.

The Real Thing

Angela Eynaud

When I was seventeen, a boy once took me to task for never phoning him. Although I was nuts about him, I'd been told by my mother that nice girls didn't phone boys; they waited for the boys to phone them. Along with this piece of sage advice came other tricks and stratagems for successfully navigating the dangerous waters of young love.

- Never chase him; boys like to do the chasing.
- Do not let him know how much you like him; keep him guessing.
- Play hard to get; boys tire of girls too easily won.

I'd stuck assiduously to these rules only to have the object of my admiration berate me, 'You're all fake. You play games. Why can't you just be real?'

I was devastated, but I owe that boy a debt of gratitude. His criticism cut deep. I have sought authenticity in relationships ever since.

I have found this difficult in church, however. So many people seem to be playing by rules which counterfeit honest communication. I have often been tempted to yell at the top of my voice, 'Why can't we just be real?'

We are least honest about our failures, struggles and brokenness.

We know from years of listening to sermons and testimonies that a Christian's life is meant to demonstrate a growth toward perfection with victory over sin, healing of past hurts and strengthening of our character. Thus when we are not whole, perfect and pure, we conclude, 'I am a failure as a Christian.' We assume everyone else is progressing along toward perfection quite nicely and they'd be scandalised to know the truth about us. It's so easy just to fake it a little and pretend to be better than we are.

The temptation is worse for those of us in leadership. We smile and say I'm fine when in reality we may only be hanging on by a thread.

I have attended Bible study groups where I was not allowed to ask difficult questions. Invariably, if I raised a contentious issue I'd be taken aside and warned about the damage my questions might be having on newer Christians. As a leader in the church I was meant to encourage faith in others. This too often meant handing out sanitised, pre-packaged answers that reduced the gospel to platitudes.

What are we afraid of? Are we afraid to ask questions in

case we find no answer? It's as if we have to be careful not to make God look bad. We have to pretend it all makes perfect sense and we have no doubts.

I once encouraged a student who was hungry to know God to ask Jesus to forgive her sins and fill her with the Holy Spirit. Alone in her room at night, in our study group and with me, she prayed over and over again. Nothing happened. When I'd prayed those prayers as a teenager, I'd had an experience of God that changed me forever, but for her . . . nothing.

I felt so frustrated and a bit embarrassed. I felt responsible for God's silence, like a stage manager who has to cover for a star's non-appearance at a promotional event. Eventually I had to confess that I had no idea why people's experience of God differed so much. I told her she'd have to trust God and allow him to deal with her however he chose. It's taken me a long time to learn the same lesson.

The Christian walk is tougher than many of us want to acknowledge. The growth toward wholeness is horribly slow. Testimonies of instant freedom from drugs or alcoholism only serve to torment us that for some God performs a quick fix while others struggle on, two steps forward, one step back.

No matter how hard we try to make God conform to our formulas and give us easy answers, he stubbornly insists on remaining God. I do not have to apologise for him or pretend to be doing better than I am so as to witness to others about the transforming power of God in my life. I'm not playing games. I want to be real.

The Girl Who Was Always Ahead

David R. Nicholas

Little Marlene was always ahead of me. No matter what I did, Marlene popped in ahead. She pipped me at the post, as it were. Sometimes I'll admit she was not very far ahead, but always she was just that fraction in front.

When I moved to another church, I lost track of Marlene. I've often wondered what happened to her.

Your curiosity has doubtless been aroused. Good. Who was Marlene? In what way was she ahead of me, and how did she accomplish such a feat?

Marlene was a small girl, nine years of age. The occasion under consideration was a Sunday school anniversary. I was the conductor. Right through the six services, whenever we sang the hymn 'Up from the grave He arose', Marlene always managed to beat everyone to the post with the first word of the chorus. 'Up!' she would fairly fling from her lips.

Little Marlene's enthusiasm knew no bounds. Always she was in front. Even during the practice prior to the anniversary, she was ahead whenever we reached that word 'Up'.

There is sadness to this story, for Marlene was handicapped insofar as she had developed slower than her school friends. This slowed development was both physical and mental. Even so, she had tremendous enthusiasm, an enthusiasm which outstripped multitudes who developed at a faster rate. Having all my mental faculties, there have been many times when I have chided myself for a lack of enthusiasm.

Enthusiasts often find themselves under fire from severe criticism, but no one dared to criticise Marlene.

Rudyard Kipling related how, on arriving at a certain port during a world tour, he watched as General Booth of the Salvation Army boarded the ship. Booth was seen off by a horde of tambourine-beating Salvationists. The whole thing revolted Kipling's sensitive soul. Later he came to know the General and told him how much he disapproved of this kind of thing. Booth said, 'Young man, if I thought that I could win one more soul for Christ by standing on my hands and beating a tambourine with my feet, I would learn to do it.'

A nine-year-old girl and the leader of the Salvation Army had one thing in common: *enthusiasm*.

Here then is the key to living the Christian life: enthusiasm in the things of God. 'Therefore, my beloved brethren, be steadfast, immovable, always abounding in the work of the Lord, knowing that your labour is not in vain in the Lord' (1 Corinthians 15:58, NKJV).

Stranger Than Fiction

John Dickson

I read somewhere, 'Fact is stranger than fiction because we write fiction to suit ourselves.'

I think this is often the case. Stories that are invented for mass consumption are usually moulded to what the public wants to hear and what it is likely to believe. True stories, on the other hand, are not invented for the public. They just happen and, because of this, are often more bizarre than anything you could make up.

Here are a few very weird examples.

- In Italy, for around $6245 you can buy ready-made coffins that have beepers, two-way speakers, a torch, a small oxygen tank, and a sensor to detect a person's heartbeat, just in case.
- To this day, in Oklahoma, USA, there is a law which forbids giving alcohol to fish.
- In Greenberry Hill, London, in 1641, three men were hanged for the murder of a local magistrate. By pure coincidence their surnames were Green, Berry and Hill.

- In the mid-1700s, the wife of a Russian peasant named Feodor Vassilyev gave birth to sixty-nine children. In twenty-seven separate pregnancies, she had sixteen pairs of twins, seven sets of triplets and four sets of quadruplets.
- In 1664, 1785 and 1860, passenger ferries sank while crossing the Menai Strait off North Wales. Amazingly, each disaster occurred on December 5. Even more bizarre, on all three occasions the name of the sole survivor was Hugh Williams.

Believe it or not, these stories are all true. They are good evidence that 'fact is often stranger than fiction'. The birth of Jesus, recorded in the original biographies, is another bizarre example of this 'stranger than fiction' principle.

Imagine you had to make up a story about God sending someone into the world to act as his ambassador, someone who was meant to show everyone what the Creator was like and how to get in touch with him (which is exactly what the biographies say of Jesus). How would *you* start the story? What sort of birth would *you* invent?

If it were up to me, I would turn it into the biggest international event in history. For starters, it would take place in one of the major cities of the world—perhaps Los Angeles, since it would be handy to have Hollywood on standby to turn it into a feature film. Just to be safe, I'd also make sure it occurred in the very best hospital in town, with all the best doctors present. The news crews of every major nation would be present, and the President of the United States would be invited to make a post-birth speech to the globe, welcoming God's ambassador to our planet. The whole thing would be beamed, via satellite, to all the cities of the world, and there could perhaps even be a live video-conference over the Internet.

Quite simply, I would make it HUGE. It would make the alien invasion in the movie *Independence Day* look like a family picnic. After all, this is meant to be *God's* ambassador. Whatever else God is, he must be big.

Silly as all this sounds, I'm just trying to illustrate that if you or I were *inventing* a story about the birth of God's ambassador, we'd at least make sure it had an air of 'importance' about it, wouldn't we?

When you read about the birth of Jesus, however, you get nothing like this. In fact, the reports of Jesus' birth are virtually the opposite of my version. Nothing you would expect to happen, happened. And many things you'd never expect to happen, did. The reports are so strange, I find it difficult to believe the authors simply invented them for popular consumption. It's as if they didn't care whether we believed them or not; they were just reporting the facts, strange as they sound.

Well then, what was so strange about the birth of Jesus? Put simply, there is very little in the story that is HUGE. Take, for example, where he is said to have been born. Here's part of the report, taken from Luke's biography:

Mary was engaged to Joseph and travelled with him to Bethlehem. She was soon going to have a baby, and while they were there, she gave birth to her firstborn son. She dressed him in baby clothes and laid him in a manger, because there was no room for them in the inn.

This is odd! Jesus was not born in a large city like Los Angeles (or even Jerusalem) but in a little country town about 10 kilometres south of Jerusalem, called 'Bethlehem'—a town about the size of Dunedoo. (Where? Exactly!) There was no fancy hospital, and it wasn't a trendy home birth. There wasn't even room in the local Bethlehem pub. As a result, Jesus ended up being born in a barn. And then, instead of being laid down in a cot, he was put in a 'manger'—an animal feeding trough. I imagine Joseph and Mary gave the trough a good clean first, but it's still a pretty rough way to come into the world. Especially if you're meant to be God's ambassador, sent to show people what God is like.

Then there's the publicity; there was hardly any. And the little there was, was pretty lame, if you ask me. Here's how Luke's account continues:

That night in the fields near Bethlehem some shepherds were guarding their sheep. All at once an angel came down to them from the Lord and said, 'I have good news for you, which will make everyone happy. This very day in King David's hometown a

Saviour was born for you. He is Christ the Lord. You will know who he is, because you will find him dressed in baby clothes and lying in a manger.' They hurried off and found Mary and Joseph, and they saw the baby lying in a manger. When the shepherds saw Jesus, they told his parents what the angel had said about him. Everyone listened and was surprised.

Admittedly, the angels must have been quite spectacular, but they are not the focus of this scene. The people entrusted with publicising God's ambassador were shepherds, and they were quite unspectacular. I mean, being a sheep-minder was not exactly a high credibility job. As I said before, if I were inventing a story about the birth of God's ambassador, I'd put some important officials at the scene, just to give it some credibility. The last people I'd leave the publicity to would be shepherds. It's no wonder people were 'surprised' when they heard what these guys had to say.

If all this is true, this is a perfect example of fact being stranger than fiction. God's ambassador, born in a shed—how bizarre!

Now, believe it or not, this strange beginning to Jesus' life is actually more significant than people often realise. If Jesus was God's ambassador, this birth story tells us something amazing about what God must be like. Let me try to explain.

When I was first introduced to Christianity, I had the idea that God was a big, powerful, great-grandfather figure, who spoke in a deep, loud voice and took pleasure using his power to boss us little humans around. But then something dawned on me. If God planned for his own ambassador to be born in a tiny town, then placed in an animal feeding trough with no one but common shepherds to witness it, what must that say about God himself?

Surely it means there must be more to God than POWER and SIZE and bossing people around. It means he must also be *humble*. It means he must have time for ordinary people. It means Jesus' visit to the planet was not just to tell us we're horrible creatures who had better get our act together. His visit must have been about getting his own hands dirty and getting alongside the little people. And as we look at the rest of Jesus' life, we discover that this is precisely what it does mean.

The man who started Buddhism, Siddhartha Gautama, was a wealthy and powerful prince; the man who started Islam, Muhammad, was a renowned and fearsome warrior. But the man who started Christianity was born in a shed. He spent most of his life unknown and ended up being executed as a criminal. At the very least, this tells us that the God Jesus represented (as ambassador) isn't out of reach or disinterested in our lives, but comes right up close. He isn't just interested in conquering the world like a grumpy old king (he could do that in a second if he wanted to) but in getting alongside it like a father or a friend.

The beginning of Jesus' life is very strange, not at all what you'd expect at the birth of God's ambassador. But as I said, fact is often stranger than fiction.

Bible quotations are adapted from Luke 2:1–20, CEV.

Removing the Jody V Millennium

Michael Frost

Recently I spent some time in the relatively remote city of Gisborne on the far east coast of the North Island of New Zealand. Surrounded by rolling green hills, the city is nestled on the flats at Poverty Bay, a large horseshoe shaped inlet that opens out to the vast South Pacific. There's nothing out there but ocean all the way to South America.

One day, a couple of weeks before my visit to town, a ship called the *Jody V Millennium*, loaded to the gunnels with timber from the nearby forests, was moored in the small harbour at the north end of Poverty Bay at the foot of the Kaiti hills. As it lay there, a ferocious storm whipped in from the Pacific. Massive waves broke more than a mile out to sea and sent walls of foaming ocean into the normally peaceful harbour. The *Jody V Millennium*, apparently safely at rest in the dock, was smashed by the surf so violently that her steel cables shattered, threatening to launch her onto the wharf and cause untold damage.

The harbour-master, foreseeing disaster, ordered the captain to put out to sea and try to dash for the other, more sheltered side of the bar. On her fateful trip across the usually idyllic Poverty Bay, the *Jody V Millennium* was pounded by the raging seas and pushed closer and closer to the beach. No matter how hard her engines tried to fight the waves, she was eventually sent reeling onto the sandy shore. Grounded, she lurched slightly to starboard and sank into the sand.

When the wind and waves finally abated the community of Gisborne awoke to an amazing sight. The enormous ship, as big as a tanker, lay stranded just off the shoreline of Waikenae Beach. When I arrived in town, the army and navy had sent helicopters to try to remove the cargo of timber logs. The Port of Melbourne Authority had sent a tugboat and salvage crew across the Tasman Sea to tow the ship out to sea. Nothing had worked. After two weeks, the *Jody V Millennium* was resolutely and embarrassingly stuck in Poverty Bay. She created quite a spectacle.

I was in town to speak at several public meetings and in various churches. My visit coincided with an exceptionally high tide, and it was believed that if ever there was a chance to shift the tanker, this was it. As I was driven through the city that Sunday afternoon, I commented to my host that the neighbourhoods seemed deserted. No one was cutting their lawn or washing their car. The main street, Gladstone Street, was empty. No children were playing in the parks or front yards. It was then we remembered that this was the afternoon that the *Jody V Millennium* was to be hauled off Waikenae Beach. We drove down to the foreshore only to encounter a traffic jam. The beachfront was jammed with cars, hot dog and meat pie vendors, and Mr Whippy ice-cream vans.

We eventually made our way through the thronging crowd to the sand dunes. The whole beach, from one end of the bay to the other, was packed with locals. Video cameras were perched on tripods sunk precariously in the sand. People gazed through binoculars and camera lenses as they observed every last detail of the salvage attempt. Children played on the sand. Strangers introduced themselves to each other.

Everyone had a theory. Some reckoned the captain had said such-and-such, others that the harbour-master had done so-and-so.

As an Australian from Sydney, a large international city, I felt this spontaneous, delightful display of community from a small, isolated city was marvellous. The *Jody V Millennium* was slowly but surely edged this way and that by the tugs until her engines coughed back into life and her propellers turned free from the sand. She powered her way out to the deep green-blue water at the centre of the bay.

Everyone complained about the expense of the exercise. 'Just think what those helicopters alone cost to get here,' they said. But from my perspective it was all money well spent. We miss out on that sense of connectivity in the regular conduct of our lives. It usually takes something bigger than ourselves to draw us together.

Awe and wonder are in rare supply these days. If a beached hulk can do it for us, imagine the impact of a collective encounter with God's majesty.

Ironically, in a city surrounded by beautiful green hills and clean, clear beaches, cliff faces and spectacular sunrises, they needed a shipping disaster to get them together on the beach one Sunday.

No Swimming!

Ken Duncan

In Kakadu, the close of the wet season makes for some beautiful photographs—and sometimes for some rather close encounters of the crocodilian kind!

Not realising this, my companion and I headed straight for some falls and leapt in. As others wandered by, we wondered why no one else saw fit to join us in the water.

Leaving the park later, we remarked how much we had enjoyed our swim. The ranger looked shocked. Hadn't we read the 'No Swimming!' signs in the camping ground? We admitted that we hadn't—that we had gone straight to the falls instead. Apparently a saltwater crocodile was still at large in the area. All efforts to trap it had failed.

Praise God for looking after us! But how often it's like that in life—we are so focused on our activities that we neglect the warning signs provided.

The Back of Bourke

Colin Buchanan

A young man swings himself from the driver's seat of a red-dusted 1970 Fairlane and slowly surveys the ramshackle collection of weathered buildings perched among the saltbush on the vast expanse of outback west of Bourke. Rewind.

Wherever you are reading this, I want you to zoom in with me. In your mind's eye, skim at 130 km/h along the dead straight stretch of baking bitumen just out of the tiny cluster of fibro, corry and brick of Byrock. A flash of grey appears on the verge and a lone roo bounds off through the scrub. The yawning cloudless outback sky arches overhead; the horizon shimmers in the distance. Mile after mile of flat red dirt and acacia gives way to mile after mile of yet more red dirt and acacia.

Finally, up ahead, the top of an old concrete water tank emerges from the western haze. Over the railway crossing—no need to look (no trains since 1989). Empty abattoir to the left. Emu and chicks pace the fence to the right. Crows wheel over the tip. 80 zone. 60 zone. Feels like walking pace after four hours of over 100 k's.

Sunday arvo. A few locals in the shade. Hook up Oxley Street. Bunch of kids playing in Central Park. But keep rolling through town, our journey's not done. Our destination is further west. Over the levee, your wheels rattle the loose bolts of the North Bourke Bridge over the Darling River. Mansell's vines to the right, take the Wanaaring Road left. Three, two, one and there goes the tar. You drop onto a stretch of dirt that winds its way, rarely interrupted by civilisation, until the continent runs out and the Indian Ocean begins, thousands of kilometres away.

Stray dust drifts in the window, gravel clatters around the wheel arch. Might just catch a country song on 2WEB before Simpson's old shearing shed looms on the left, a random smattering of outbuildings and the welcoming arms of the old Kurrajong trees. We're there. Up the drive and pull up. Engine off. The scorching exhaust clicks as it cools. Swing open the door. Thonged foot lands in a smooth patch of fine red dust, leaving a perfect, beachcomber double plugged print. One small step for a man . . .

It's 1988 and that fella in the matching Mambo boardies and T-shirt is me. Swapping the best part of a lifetime in the Sydney 'burbs for a caravan in a shed at Pera Bore. Challenged eight months earlier on a verandah about 150 yards from where I'm now standing by a sharp-minded boy from Yackandandah.

'Seems to me, Colin, that you need to make your mind up whether you're going to seek first the kingdom of God or not.'

So my wife of eighteen months, Robyn, and I had made up our minds to take up residence for two years in a Chesney caravan at Cornerstone Christian Community, and there I was, compelled by the desire to follow Christ, setting off on an adventure to let the yeast of belonging to Christ spread through the whole of my life. I'd just taken the first step on an adventure that, fifteen years later, is still unfolding.

'Seek first the kingdom of God and his righteousness.' Jesus' words are so grand, so huge, so life-wide. But I remember that drive to Bourke, and I love replaying that moment because it was such a significant small step for me in obeying the Saviour's call. It wasn't the first step and won't be the last. In fact, that's really my point.

The adventure of walking with Jesus sets apart the collection of circumstances and decisions and friendships and thoughts and experiences of a life, whether large or small, public or private, monumental or minuscule. Sets them apart as his. And a monumental moment of spiritual breakthrough can seem to anyone looking on as nothing more than . . . a drive to Bourke?

If Jesus is your Master, give him the length and breadth of who you are and what you would become. But start with the next insignificant, minuscule moment. Like my drive to Bourke, it may become a moment you'll never forget.

Breakfast and Blessing

Darlene Zschech

One day I was lying in bed when my daughter Chloe said, 'Mummy, sit up, sit up, I want to make you breakfast.' She was five at the time, so it was a fairly 'out there' thought that I was going to have to eat something she produced!

She had watched me and knew I liked to eat this toast that looks like horse food (it's supposed to be healthy for you). But she's not allowed to use the toaster. We keep the bread in the freezer, so the bread was frozen—rock hard. She just popped it on a tray, then she called out, 'Sit up, Mum, I'm nearly ready.'

I also drink herbal tea, but she's not allowed to use the kettle. So she got a cup out of the cupboard and put a teabag in it with cold water. And then—and I don't know where this came from—a squashed banana (I think that was from her past or something).

Anyway, she's all ready, and here it comes: 'Sit up, Mum,

I'm coming, I'm coming.' I was sitting up (praying!) and in she walked, so very proud of herself. 'Are you sitting up? I've got your breakfast!' And she put it in my lap.

Words failed me.

'Do you love it, Mum?'

'Yep, I sure do.'

I waited for her to leave, but she didn't. She just sat on my bed, looking at me with the cutest of expressions. And suddenly I knew: *I had to eat this!*

So what does every good mother do? We eat it.

'Mmmmm, Chloe, it's beautiful!'

The look on her face was priceless.

Chloe didn't make me breakfast to win points with me. She was too young to know that there might be money attached. All she wanted to do was to bless me.

That kind of breakfast is not what she is going to be able to bring me one day. But for that day, she gave me her best. She just gave what she had with a heart that was very pure and wanted to bless her mum.

If you feel like you have nothing to offer God, nothing to bring to the table, you need to know that God doesn't want what you are going to be, or what you can see you'd like to be. He just wants all that you are today. You bring that in worship, you bring that in praise, you let that explosion of faith force you to praise His name . . . and just bring what you have.

Do you think it will bless the heart of God? Hey, Chloe blessed me! I'm still talking about it. And you will bless the heart of God because he looks past all the stuff of life and straight to the heart.

Overcoming Entropy

Amanda Smith

All around me dust is falling
Stomachs are emptying
Cobwebs are amassing
Mildew is multiplying
Food is decaying
Dirty dishes are gathering

The Second Law of Thermodynamics states that
You cannot break even
You cannot return to the same energy state,
Because there is always an increase in disorder;
Entropy always increases.

If it weren't for me, there would be chaos.

My work is the kind
That is only noticed when it's not done.
No one says, 'Oh Look!
There's no vomit in the carpet,
No Play-Doh in the VCR,
No clog in the toilet,
And my drawer is full of clean underwear!'

But I spend my days accomplishing these marvels of physics,
Depleting Energy
But
Overcoming Entropy.

The Day Christ Stopped the Bulldozers

Dave Andrews

If people adopt the agenda of God, personified in Christ, as the agenda for their decision-making, they have made a significant transition. The agenda of God has moved from being a point of view to the point of reference. The process of conversion to Christ as a person—not necessarily Christianity as a religion—has begun. And part and parcel of this conversion process is its incredible potential for authentic, sustainable community transformation.

Let me tell you a story of how such a process took place among a group of people who were not only non-Christians, but decidedly anti-Christian ...

When I was living in India years ago, some friends and I decided to get involved with a bunch of squatters. They were totally demoralised. They had no jobs. With no jobs they could not afford to pay rent. Because they had nowhere to live they squatted on land beside the road. Because this was illegal, they were constantly harassed by the police, who would either demand a bribe or break down their huts and beat them up. As a result they were constantly on the move, trying desperately to stay one step ahead of the police. But there weren't many places they could go, so they always wound up back where they started, ready to go through the cycle again.

We got to know this group. Bonds of friendship formed between individuals and their families. What they lacked in dignity, they more than made up for in guts. Their struggle against seemingly overwhelming odds was fought with lots of courage and lots of laughter. We were encouraged and strengthened by their infectious style of heroism and sense of humour.

They may have been demoralised, but they taught us valuable lessons about morality. As our friendships deepened, we not only learned from them the art of survival in an urban slum, we began to feel the anguish they felt in their struggle. As we discussed with them the issues they had to face every day of their lives, we decided to work with them and see if together we could find some long-term solutions that would not only minimise the anguish associated with their struggle for survival, but also increase their chances.

One day the group decided something had to be done about the continuing police harassment. Some wanted to attack the police station immediately with bricks. Bricks were a common means of settling disputes in the slum. As a conflict resolution technique the people considered it a knockout. We encouraged them to envisage in their minds what the result of throwing bricks through the window of the police station might be. They concluded that it would probably result in an even more violent visit by the police. They began to have very serious doubts about the effectiveness of bricks as a conflict resolution technique.

So we began to discuss other possibilities for solving the problem. Someone suggested inviting the police over for a cup or tea and discussing the matter. The squatters treated the idea with scorn, but we supported it. The longer we discussed it, the more support it got.

Eventually the police were invited. To start with, you could have cut the air with a knife, but the tension was soon dispelled with a couple of jokes. The squatters and the police ended up having an amicable chat and as a result decided to call a truce. The squatters agreed not to cause the police any trouble and the police agreed not to beat up the squatters.

After the police had gone, we had a talk about how the problem had been resolved. During the discussion one of us mentioned that the problem had been resolved exactly the way Christ had suggested such problems be resolved. He said, 'Bless those who curse you' and 'If your enemy is thirsty give him a drink', which is exactly what the group had done by inviting the police for a cup of tea. Everyone treated it as a joke. They were embarrassed that they had done anything remotely religious, even if unintentionally. But the squatters remembered the way they had solved the problem with the police, and they also remembered that it was the way Christ suggested problems be solved.

Time went by. Week after week, month after month, we worked on a whole range of problems together, everything from getting a regular water supply to improving nutrition and sanitation. Each time we resolved a problem together it would be on the basis of common sense and consensus. After the effective resolution of each of these problems, we would discuss how the decision we had taken fitted with the way Christ advocated that problems be dealt with. After each successful resolution of a problem there would be a celebration. It was during this euphoria that we would always explain how the success was contingent upon our having worked in harmony with God's agenda, as personified in Christ; and always there would be the mock groans that if we carried on the way we were going, they would all be Christians before too long!

About a year after inviting the police for a cup of tea, the city council decided to clean up the city. Cleaning up the city meant getting rid of the squatters. They were notified to leave immediately. But they had nowhere to go. Then they got some news that really freaked them out. The bulldozers were on the way. In a panic they considered their options. There didn't seem to be any. Any promising options had to be discarded because the people felt too powerless to make them happen. 'It's typical,' they concluded. 'Those big people can push us little people around as much as they like and there is not a thing we can do about it.'

We were tempted to agree. Things looked hopeless. But somehow we knew that we had to believe the impossible was possible. 'Surely there is *something* we can do!' one person said hopefully. 'Yeah?' asked one of the squatters. 'What? What would Christ do about it?'

Raising Christ as a possible point of reference for solving a problem had never happened before in our discussions with the squatters. It was a crucial time for this group—a time when Christ might become more than just one point of view among many points of view; a time when Christ might become the point of reference for all their problem-solving, when the group might be converted to a faith in Christ through which their life might be transformed. It all hinged upon finding a Christ story that the group could use to help them *do* something about their situation. I racked my brain, wondering where on earth you could find a story in the Gospels that might help a group of squatters deal with the threat of eviction backed by the might of bulldozers.

I don't remember who it was, but someone suggested a story they thought might help. It was the story Christ told of a little old widow who was finding it difficult to get justice from a big crooked judge. She finally got justice by knocking on his door at all hours of the night for week after week.

As we discussed the story with the squatters, hope began to rise out of their hopelessness. As hope was born, so was a new sense of power. They started discussing the possible solutions in a whole new light. They decided to take up a petition to present to city council and to persist until they got a fair hearing. They gathered hundreds of signatures and organised a march to the city council administration centre to present the petitions. Then they followed up on the people who could change the decision. Finally, through the kind of perseverance they had learned about in the story of the little old widow, they were granted an alternative place to stay where the community would have their own houses on their own land. Not only that; the council would help pay the expenses of their move. It was more than they had ever dreamed possible.

The move also opened up a whole host of new doors. Now they had their own homes on their own land, they could develop their own education, health and employment programs. With the decrease in demoralisation came an observable increase in morale—and morality—in the community. There was a marked decrease in domestic violence and child abuse. People engaged in more constructive forms of work, and less destructive forms of recreation. There was a marked increase in happier couples and healthier children. Fewer people went to untimely graves. And those who survived not only lived longer but also lived fuller lives.

And at the centre of all this activity was a group in the community who remembered that the personal growth and social change had come about because they had followed the agenda of God, personified in Christ. This group weren't content with their growth so far. They looked into the future and saw some of the changes that were possible—if they followed in the footsteps of Christ and, like him, lived wholeheartedly for God, and his agenda of love and justice.

Hedonists Don't Get No Satisfaction

Grenville Kent

'My ultimate fantasy is to watch a shopping channel, with a credit card, while making love and eating at the same time.' So says Yasmine Bleeth, *Baywatch* Babe (and part-time philosopher).

I guess that's one way to get a man to come shopping. But imagine: 'I only have eyes for bruschetta, you and that Prada handbag.'

'Huh? I was watching the football.'

But for many people, she's expressed the meaning of life—pleasure. If you believe the advertising media, it's the things we own, wear, consume and sleep with that are our life. We are what we buy. Purpose and identity traditionally come from spirituality, so marketing must be the new religion, preaching salvation by spending and a secular heaven on earth.

Economics professor Jeremy Rifkin says, 'The advertisers and market leaders have become the gatekeepers of human experience who alone can tell us where happiness, spirituality and hope may be found at free market prices.'

Money is my shepherd, I shall not want.
It maketh me to lie down in five-star comfort;
It leadeth me in the paths of hedonism;
It restoreth my self-esteem.
It can buy me love (or a fair imitation).
Yea, though I walk alone, I shall spend like the beautiful people,
Thy Amex and Visa, they creature-comfort me,
And I will dwell in pleasure all my 2600 weekends. (Psalm $22.99)

Except that it doesn't work. *Time* recently published a study that showed the world's happiest country was not the USA, Switzerland or anywhere else rich and glamorous. It was Bangladesh! One of the world's poorest countries, it is also one of the most connected and relational.

The problem with pleasure is that all the graphs head downward eventually. I know; I'm a failed hedonist. And no, I'm not writing this from the Betty Ford Clinic—they don't deal with guacamole addictions. Hear my cautionary tale.

On a recent north coast holiday, my wife Carla and I came upon a roadside stall selling luscious avocados, cheap. We're both avocado addicts and drove away with half a boot-load.

Dinner that night was a to-die-for avocado salad—avocado, tomato and lettuce. Breakfast was toast topped with avocado lightly fried in garlic—angel food. Lunch was avocado sandwiches with fillings four centimetres thick. Dinner was guacamole on corn chips. We were in heaven!

The next day was just as good, but the following morning we looked at each other and at the green ripening pile on our bench. 'We'd better use them up,' I said without enthusiasm. We realised we'd gone from surfing the very pinnacle of the pleasure curve down to jaded toleration. By dinner that night, I couldn't do it anymore. I started giving away bags of avocados. Suddenly I was a generous person.

Carla and I had discovered what economists term the Law of Diminishing Marginal Returns (DMR). Simply put, it states: 'Everything starts great, but soon it sucks.'

DMR applies to chocolate mudcake. The first slice might be worth $10 if you're hungry. The second slice? Say $8. Then maybe $5, then $3. But when you're full it's worth $0. If you're overstuffed, you'd pay $10 not to eat more, so your graph is into negative values.

DMR applies to heroin too. I'm told the first shot is bliss, but then you need it just to feel normal, and then you drop into hell. DMR also applies to shopping. Women even tire of that—or so I've read.

Maybe the law of DMR is God's built-in limiter on lust and selfishness, a reminder not to forget our souls and other people. 'Too much of a good thing can be wonderful,' said Mae West, another generation's babe. But she was wrong.

Pleasure is eventually a downward graph, however high you start. Look at the sad lives of so many stars.

And pleasure is no test of truth. Someone said, 'Why do I need rules? I have nerves.' But we need principles other than the pleasure principle. 'If it feels good, do it' is no way to run the world.

True hedonists believe in the 'enlightened pursuit of pleasure'—making the lollipop last, not spoiling tomorrow's pleasure by overdoing it today. But the Rolling Stones have had thirty-five years of every party, chemical substance and groupie known, and they still 'Can't Get No Satisfaction' (though they try, and they try, hey-hey). Mick Jagger's ex-wife, Jerry Hall, says she feels 'sorry' for the multi-squillionaire rocker: 'Sexual promiscuity just leads to chaos . . . I wish he'd find happiness.'

'Eat, drink and be merry, for tomorrow we die,' said the ancient Epicureans who met the Christian teacher Paul. But he told them about Jesus and the resurrection (Acts 17:18)—Jesus because he said that anyone who really wants to live this life should throw their selfishness away (that's a paradox, and I wonder whether even Christians believe him); and resurrection because it promises an afterlife where you never get old or blasé, and satisfaction curves go upwards forever.

Economist J. K. Galbraith said, 'In the long run, we're all dead.' But not if you know God.

Paul was quite scornful of Christians who live hedonistically:

'Whoever lives for pleasure is dead while they're alive.' Dead? Yes, at least in spirit. Martin Luther King said, 'An individual has not started living until he can rise above the narrow confines of his individualistic concerns to the broader concerns of all humanity ... Every man must decide whether he will walk in the light of creative altruism or the darkness of destructive selfishness. This is the judgment. Life's most persistent and urgent question is, What are you doing for others?'

Nothing against food or sex (although I hate shopping). But, Yasmine, if you want to exit the mall of selfish superficiality and be happy for longer than thirty minutes, try chasing spirituality and generous relationships.

Bible quotations are paraphrases drawn from Luke 17:33; 1 Corinthians 15:32; 1 Timothy 5:6.

The Truth Versus the Facts

Christine Caine

The truth of God's Word is always more powerful than the 'facts' of our circumstances. Our eternal destiny is always determined by the truth of the Word of God. The facts are often contrary to the truth.

I was confronted by this reality through my adoption and subsequent search for my biological mother.

When I discovered, at the age of thirty-two, that I had been adopted, I actually needed several months to get used to the idea that I had a different biological mother to my brother. I had no overwhelming desire to contact this woman. Although she had given birth to me, she was a stranger and had played no part in my life.

I was travelling continuously during this time and had many opportunities to share about my adoption. After each meeting, I ended up speaking to many people who had either been adopted or had given up a child for adoption.

I found myself lying awake at night wondering what my

story was. Eventually I contacted the adoption centre and filled in the forms to start the search for my biological mother. Soon after, I received my birth certificate and hospital records.

I was a little nervous as I opened the envelope at home alone. I pulled out my original birth certificate. This was a somewhat interesting experience, given that I had been married, and obtained a passport and other official documents, with what I had always thought to be my original birth certificate.

My biological mother's name was recorded on the form; however, in the box next to father's name was the word 'unknown'. Even more devastating was what appeared next to the box where my name should have been: 'UNNAMMED'.

My heart sank. I stood in my kitchen sobbing as I held this piece of paper, feeling so alone, rejected and abandoned.

My mind was filled with many thoughts. I wondered why this woman who had carried me in her womb for nine months did not want me. Why did she not even name me? Was I conceived out of love or at a party one drunken night? Or was I the result of a rape?

As I sat crouched over and crying, God reminded me of his Word.

> *The Lord has called me from the womb; from the body of my mother He has named my name. (Isaiah 49:1, AMP)*

At that point I grabbed my Bible. With it in one hand, and my birth certificate in the other, I had a choice to make. Was I going to accept the facts that appeared on my birth certificate or the truth contained in the Word of God?

I was able to find comfort in the fact that God's Word revealed the Truth concerning my conception and life plan.

For You did form my inward parts; You did knit me together in my mother's womb. I will confess and praise You for You are fearful and wonderful and for the awful wonder of my birth! Wonderful are Your works, and that my inner self knows right well. My frame was not hidden from You when I was being formed in secret [and] intricately and curiously wrought [as if embroidered with various colors] in the depths of the earth [a region of darkness and mystery]. Your eyes saw my unformed substance, and in Your book all the days [of my life] were written before ever they took shape, when as yet there was none of them. (Psalm 139:13–16, AMP)

God was there from the moment of my conception. In fact, before I was ever conceived, I existed in eternity. I can be confident in my future because of Jesus Christ. I may not be who I thought I was, *but I am who he says I am.*

God in the Strip Club

Michael Frost

One day, after an evangelistic campaign, a beautiful young woman approached evangelist John Smith and begged him to come and meet her. She had been deeply moved by what he had said and needed to talk further.

John sadly explained that he needed to go quickly to his next speaking engagement and couldn't spare the time right then. But she was so insistent in her need to find out more about Jesus that he agreed to meet with her later that night. She thrust a piece of paper in his hand, asking him to meet her at that address, and ran off.

When he checked the note later, he realised she had arranged to meet him at one of the city's most notorious strip clubs.

This put John in a bit of a dilemma. It is his normal practice that whenever he is entering edgy places, he always takes another member of his team. But John thought this could well be a set up by one of the sleaze newspapers to take a photo of one of Australia's leading evangelists going into a strip joint, so he decided to go alone. (Whatever you might think of the wisdom of that choice, I ask you to withhold your judgment and get to the core of the story.)

That night he arrived at the striptease club, found a table and asked the waitress to get Linda (not her real name). When the waitress returned she brought him a drink, but not Linda. He told her he had been asked to meet Linda there that night and the waitress, still not believing the story, asked for his name. When he told her, she replied, 'Yeah, sure, everyone in this place is John Smith.'

Eventually he persuaded her to get Linda. When she arrived she thanked John profusely for coming and began to tell the story of her life.

She had always loved dancing and always wanted to be a performer. At seventeen she met a young Christian guy and fell in love. He took her to hear John at his church (called Truth and Liberation Concern in Melbourne) and that day she became a Christian. However, her boyfriend came from an ultra-conservative denomination that looked down on all forms of worldliness, especially dancing, and his parents forced him to end their relationship. Linda had been forced to choose between dancing and him, and she chose dancing.

This devastated Linda because she quite rightly associated Jesus with the actions of his people—in this case, his exceedingly narrow people. Subsequently she gave up on the church and her faith and devoted herself to a career in dancing.

Life didn't go all that well for her, though. She could get no jobs, dancing or otherwise, and against her better judgment ended up stripping for a living. She claimed that at least she could dance and the money was good. It was the story of so many in that sad industry.

As they talked about her family, her dreams, Jesus and the meaning of things, Linda felt it was time for her to come back to Jesus. John led her back to Christ right there in the club.

This might have been the end of a simple story of a young woman's journey back to Jesus, but for the strange twist at the end of the tale. When it came time for her to strip again, she turned to the man who had just prayed a prayer of re-commitment with her and asked him to stay and watch her dance. Not many evangelists find themselves in this situation because most of them do their preaching in churches. Here was Australia's leading evangelist being begged by a recent convert to watch her routine.

John thought this was taking things a bit far, but again Linda prevailed and he stayed for the dance. (Again I ask you to withhold your moral judgment here; John has always kept a rigorous accountability in these things and sees himself as an ambassador of Christ in the toughest of places.)

Linda did her dance. The choice of the song was 'Only Seventeen' by Janis Ian, a song about rejection and being an 'ugly duckling'. She had woven the story of her loss of faith into her strip act.

Now the question John asks—and which I now ask you—is this: was Jesus in the strip club that night? You must attempt an answer here. Can God be found in that place of tragedy and brokenness? I believe that to be biblical you must answer yes.

The question that follows is the key missional one. If God was in that place, wooing Linda to himself through Jesus Christ, was it all right for John to join him in mission in that place, in the act of redeeming a broken life? Had God prepared the soil, caused the sun to shine and the rain to fall? Had God arranged the situation so that John might watch that striptease and lead that woman away from sin and into wholeness?

The answer I leave to you. I reckon you can guess mine.

My Escape from the World Trade Centre

Hans Kunnen

At 8.51 a.m. on September 11, 2001, I was sitting in a room on the ground floor of the World Trade Centre Marriott Hotel. I was attending the National Association of Business Economists Conference. The hotel was at the base of the North Tower, one of seven buildings that comprised the World Trade Centre.

When the first plane hit, all we felt was a dull thud, then a moment later the sound of a seemingly distant explosion. I thought it was an earthquake as the lights and tables shook. Within moments, people headed for the doors, running for their lives.

Whimps, I thought. *What's the matter with them?*

I didn't recall it at that moment, but it wasn't the first time the complex had been the object of a terrorist attack. Within a minute or two, there were only three of us left in the room. We wandered out to see what had happened.

As I entered the hotel lobby, dishevelled and frightened

people streamed into the foyer, seeking shelter. They were in shock, and some had obviously been injured by falling debris and burning jet fuel from the impact of American Airlines Flight 11.

I knew I was in the midst of a disaster and that this was the end of my stay, so I went to a lift to go to my room on the sixth floor and retrieve my luggage. But the alarms were sounding, and I was refused entry and politely asked to leave the complex.

Just after 9.00 a.m., I walked outside in the direction of the Hudson River. As I exited, I was greeted by a shower of burning paper swirling in the wind across a streetscape that resembled a war zone. And indeed, that's what it was. Everything in sight was strewn with rubble, debris and burning cars.

I walked across Liberty Street, between the two World Financial Centre buildings about 200 metres away, and looked back to where smoke belched from the stricken, doomed North Tower. As I gasped in awe at the horror, the air was filled with the deafening roar of jet engines. I watched, horrified and disbelieving, as another plane, United Airlines Flight 175, slammed into the upper floors of the South Tower behind my hotel. Flames, smoke and glass erupted. Bodies and debris were blown out of the building and rained down on the street.

From that moment, I did not look back. It was time to get

away. My mind raced: *Were more planes coming? Where would safety be found?*

I'd taken the Staten Island ferry from Battery Point, about 700 metres south, on the previous Saturday, so I fast-walked to the wharf. It seemed the best alternative at the time. There I joined thousands of others attempting to escape the carnage and whatever else might be about to follow. Suddenly, just as the ferry boarding gates opened, behind me came a thunderous noise.

People screamed. We thought the city was being attacked yet again, and this time I thought I might die. It was the South Tower collapsing. As we took our places on the ferry, smoke, ash and dust billowed toward us, enveloping us. People donned life jackets.

As a Christian I thought I would be welcomed if I knocked on the door of a church in Staten Island and asked for help. But amazingly, and in the altered spirit of care and goodwill that immediately enveloped New Yorkers in the wake of the tragedy, a complete stranger standing near me on the ferry asked me and two other people to join her family at their home until things were sorted out. Her name was Leslie Castelucci. The Casteluccis and their neighbours gave me clothing and took me in as if I were a close family member. I weep as I remember her act of kindness.

Meanwhile, my wife, Suzanne, was at home in Sydney. She was preparing for bed when her mother alerted her to what was happening soon after the first plane hit. In the cold, dark hours following, she watched live on television as the second plane hit and the towers collapsed. Our three young children, thankfully, remained asleep, unaware of my peril.

Suzanne, of course, knew I was in New York, and vaguely recalled me mentioning the World Trade Centre as my destination. She rang some work colleagues to ask, and they confirmed the conference location. When she heard nothing from me, she began to fear the worst. A friend came round to keep her company, and she and others prayed for my safety. But mostly she sat in silent horror and watched the drama and its aftermath replayed over and again on television.

I knew I was safe, but she didn't. It was almost four hours after the attack before I was able to contact her, at about 2.30 a.m. Sydney time. The day was bad for me, but for Suzanne it was a nightmare.

Two days later I headed back into Manhattan, to a hotel close to the Australian consulate. I'd lost my passport, airline tickets, cash, clothing and other personal effects in the inferno, although fortunately I still had my wallet.

But even that journey wasn't without drama. Paranoia and extraordinary scrutiny were apparent everywhere. As my bus approached the New Jersey Turnpike, a major artery into Manhattan, it was halted in a traffic jam. We were told to demount and find our own way to the city.

Just as I alighted, a police car with sirens screaming pulled over a car just 20 metres from me. Three policemen jumped out and ordered the driver out, holding a shotgun under his nose. Just above the suburban rooftops, a police chopper hovered. It was like a scene from a police drama. Having survived September 11, I didn't want to die in a shoot-out with either a car thief or a terrorist, so I ducked behind a big green Lincoln. But within a few minutes the hapless motorist (he must have inadvertently run a road block) was released and we all went on our way.

With the bus a no-goer, I switched my mode of transport to rail, eventually making it to Grand Central Station, the world's largest, in the middle of Manhattan. Again I was met by police, this time with megaphones, asking us not to panic but to leave the building as there was a bomb threat in the station. As if my nerves weren't frayed enough.

Having organised a new passport and bought a few new clothes, I waited for the airport to reopen. I gave blood. I went to church, wandered through Central Park and watched television. I cried and I prayed. But I also dwelt on Psalm 25 and thanked God for his safe-keeping.

New York was a hurt and sorrowing place, and I was looking forward to getting home. But it was a week before I finally flew into Sydney and, with tears flowing once again, wrapped my arms around my much-relieved family.

What do I make of it all now, in retrospect? I've come to appreciate that any minute might be my last. And if that's the case, I recognise the continuing need to 'be right' at all times with my family, my friends and most of all with God. Also, and without being crippled by constant morbid thoughts, I'm now more caring toward others and try to make the most of opportunities I'm afforded.

On September 11, 2001, I almost lost my life, my wife and my children. But I realise that, in this dangerous and uncertain world where everyone, even children it seems, is a target, I could lose them tomorrow. So every day I thank God for them. Despite my busy and demanding career, I try to give them all more of my attention and time.

Meeting the Godfather

Grenville Kent

December 22. Peace and goodwill were still three days away. Sydney's drivers sweated as the demons of capitalism drove them on to one more project before the fat man slid down the chimney.

I was taking my computer for psychoanalysis, worrying whether I could extract two weeks' worth of film editing from its troubled mind. I pushed through baking traffic that flowed like a bachelor's custard.

Suddenly brake lights in front lit up like a Christmas tree. As my foot reacted, my brain knew it was pointless and idly admired the gleaming BMW 740, wide radials, computer-controlled braking system . . . ka-thump! Hello BMW. Bye-bye Christmas savings fund.

The Bee-Em's door burst open and an Italian gentleman wearing a shiny, dark suit jumped out and paced toward me, punching his palm and yelling, 'I'm a gonna kill him.'

Santa Sophia! I'd hit the Godfather. My concrete shoe size is twelve. Tell my wife I love her.

'I'm gonna kill that fettuccini!' (he didn't say fettuccini, but it alliterates).

His wife and two big sons were also getting out. If it came to violence, I'd have lasted thirty seconds—less if the men helped her.

'We got the fettuccini's rego, huh, boys?' said the Godfather. 'Yes, Dad,' they nodded gravely. 'My lawyer's gonna eat that fettuccini. He cuts into my lane, stops, causes an accident, then drives off!'

Drives off? Oh, he must be talking about the ute driver who made him brake. I'm not the fettuccini! Relief! But I was still in the wrong. I walked up and said, 'Hi. Sorry about this. It's clearly my fault.' I handed him my card and showed him my licence. He followed suit.

'Let's have a look,' he said.

My grill was broken, my bumper pointing at the sky. His bumper was made of some high-tech flubber and seemed quite undamaged. He bent down for a closer look and we finally spotted a tiny dent, no wider or deeper than a fingernail. But his car was immaculate and he had to consider resale value. His new bumper would be worth more than my whole car. (No kidding, I checked.)

He looked at me hard, then put out his hand to shake mine. 'Ah, look . . . Merry Christmas'. His tanned face broke into a smile that would have charmed anyone from here to Firenze.

'Happy Christmas,' I grinned, barely believing my luck, reminded of the ultimate God Father's generosity and kindness about our dumbest and meanest mistakes.

I remembered the baby born to pay for the sins of the world, becoming the world's fettuccini and dying so that we can live. 'Happy Christmas, Mrs Leotta, gentlemen.' La Familia nodded and smiled with amazing peace and goodwill.

Happy Christmas to you, too. Grab the outstretched hand of our smiling God. Oh, and drive carefully.

'Stop and appreciate this amazing God ... who has visited and saved his people ... by forgiving their sins, through his tender mercy ... The brightest Star in the universe has orbited here, to give His people knowledge of how to be saved, to give light to those who sit in darkness and the shadow of death, and to guide our feet in a path of peace' (Luke 1:68–79, my paraphrase).

Contributors

Dave Andrews went to India in 1973 with his wife, Ange, to set up an open home for junkies, drop-outs and other disturbed people in Delhi. They subsequently founded a community for Indians which they ran until they were forced to leave India in 1984. Back in Australia, they began working with dispossessed people in Brisbane, including Aborigines, refugees and the mentally disturbed. Dave is the author of several books including *Christi-Anarchy* (Lion, 1999) and *Not Religion, But Love* (Lion, 2001).

Philip Baker is the Senior Minister of Riverview Church in Perth, one of Australia's largest churches, with an average Sunday attendance of over 2500. He is also President of Australian Christian Churches, a growing alliance of 1200 churches throughout the country. Philip and his team produce the television program *ChurchLIVE@Riverview*, seen in Australia, New Zealand, Africa and Europe. He is the author of several books including *Attitudes of Amazing Achievers* (Webb & Partners, 2000).

Nathan Brown is a freelance writer, based in Townsville, Queensland, where he is also working on a PhD in English at James Cook University.

Colin Buchanan is one of Australia's best-loved entertainers. The winner of six Golden Guitar awards, he is well-known for his popular country songs, his series of best-selling children's CDs and his appearances as a regular on ABC TV's *Playschool*. He lives in Sydney with his wife Robyn and their four children.

Geoff Bullock is a popular songwriter whose songs of worship are sung throughout the world. His best-known song is 'The Power of Your Love', and his book of the same name was honoured by the Australian Christian Literature Society with a commendation in 2001. Geoff is also the bestselling author of *Hands of Grace* (Strand Publishing, 1998).

Christine Caine is the director of Equip & Empower Ministries and Coordinator of Hillsong Network, based in Sydney. One of Australia's busiest Christian speakers, she is the author of three books including *Youth Ministry: Principles for the 21st Century* (Equip & Empower Resources, 2000). She and her husband Nick live in inner Sydney and have one daughter.

Margaret Court is a tennis legend who dominated the game in the 1960s and early '70s, winning more Grand Slam titles than anyone else in history. Margaret is now the pastor of a thriving church in Perth and the bestselling author of

Winning Words and *Winning Faith* (Strand Publishing, 1999, 2000).

John Dickson's warm and humorous books about Christianity have been best-sellers throughout Australia and the UK. John has a busy life speaking about the Christian message in churches, schools and universities all over his native Sydney and beyond. Just for fun, he has recently completed a PhD in ancient history. According to him, however, his finest achievements are marrying Elizabeth and raising Joshua and Sophie. (For more information on John's books, including *A Sneaking Suspicion, Hanging In There, A Hell of a Life, Simply Christianity: Beyond Religion* and *If I Were God, I'd End All the Pain*, visit matthiasmedia.com.au)

Sue Duggan is a freelance writer who lives on the Central Coast of New South Wales. Sue is married to Mike and has two children, Catherine and Peter.

Ken Duncan is one of the world's leading exponents of panoramic landscape photography. Ken sees himself as 'an average photographer with a great God'—a man with a passion to show others the beauty of God's creation. Ken's latest books are *Australia Wide* and *Classic Australia*. His online gallery can be found at www.kenduncan.com

Angela Eynaud teaches English, Literature and History at Northside Christian College in Melbourne. Her pleasures are books, art and theatre, and she dreams of writing a great novel. She worships at St Mark's Anglican Church, Reservoir, where she leads a team that runs an outreach service, making extensive use of creative arts and multimedia. She and her husband Stephen have two sons.

Dudley Foord has served in a wide range of ministries: parish minister, theological lecturer and overseas missionary. He spent four years as presiding bishop of the Church of England in South Africa and Zimbabwe. The Men's Katoomba Convention, which today draws 8000 men, began in 1996 under his chairmanship. Dudley and his wife, Elizabeth, now exercise a ministry as church consultants and itinerant Bible teachers, travelling in Australia, Africa and Asia. They have four children and eleven grandchildren.

Michael Frost is the vice principal at Morling College and the founding director of the Centre for Evangelism and Global Mission at Morling. He is the author of a number of books including *Eyes Wide Open* (Albatross, 1998) and *Lessons from Reel Life* (Open Book, 2001). He is a much sought after conference speaker around Australia.

Mal Garvin is the founder and national director of the national youth and community organisation Fusion Australia. In 1995 Mal established a therapeutic community for needy young people and a training school for youth and community workers, both now located at Poatina, Tasmania, where Mal lives and works. The author of three books, he is in great demand as a speaker for conferences, seminars and forums exploring human communication and social processes. His daily radio program 'Breakthru' and weekly magazine program 'Sunday Night with Mal Garvin' are heard on over forty radio stations across Australia.

Steve Grace is a well-known Australian singer/songwriter with a heart for world evangelism. In 1987, when he was driving trucks on the central coast of New South Wales, he answered the call of God and pioneered a concert ministry that has taken him to hundreds of regional towns and cities around Australia, serving local churches in their task of evangelism and exciting Christians about mission. He describes his ministry as an adventure led by God, strongly supported with huge steps of faith from his family and team. (Website: www.stevegrace.com)

Kim Hawtrey lives in Sydney and is a Christian speaker with Impact Evangelism. His books include *First Impression* (Aquila Press, 1994) and *The True and Living God* (Matthias Media, 1998). Kim likes 'slow food' and enjoys communicating 'offline'. He is married to Jenny and they have four daughters.

Phillip Jensen is a chaplain at the University of New South Wales and minister of St Matthias Anglican Church, Centennial Park, Sydney. He is a well-known Bible teacher, is married to Helen and has three children.

Philip Johnson is adjunct lecturer in Old Testament at Morling Baptist College, and visiting lecturer in cults and world religions at the Presbyterian Theological Centre,

Sydney. He is co-author with Ross Clifford of *Riding the Rollercoaster* (Strand Publishing, 1998) and *Jesus and the Gods of the New Age* (Lion, 2001). He is also the CEO of Global Apologetics & Mission, a ministry that specialises in outreach to other faiths.

Grenville Kent has worked as a writer and filmmaker, and now pastors Chatswood Adventist, a church of young adults. He has just completed a book, *God on Sex*, and is working on a documentary about views of the afterlife. He and his wife, Carla, have two children.

Jonathan Krause has worked at World Vision for thirteen years after previous 'lives' as a pastry-chef, church worker, window-washer and Australia's only full-time writer of verses for greeting cards. He has visited more than twenty countries for World Vision writing about its life-saving work. He has also been manager of the organisation's Youth Department and National Manager of the 40 Hour Famine. Jonathan is married with an eighteen-year-old son and ten-year-old daughter.

Hans Kunnen is head of Investment Markets Research for Colonial First State Investments in Sydney. Prior to joining Colonial First State, he was chief economist for the State Bank of New South Wales, and also spent time teaching economics at Macquarie University. He and his wife, Suzanne, have three children and attend Oakhill Family Church in Sydney, a branch church of St Paul's Anglican Church in Castle Hill.

John Mallison is a Uniting Church minister. He is an internationally-known Christian educator who has conducted leadership development events in twenty-nine countries and authored twenty-two books. He now devotes himself almost entirely to modelling, teaching and promoting mentoring.

Max Meyers is Vice President at Large for Development Associates International, an organisation involved in developing senior Christian leaders throughout the Third World. After a career as a fighter pilot with the RAAF, he flew for Mission Aviation Fellowship for nearly twenty-four years, holding various leadership roles before becoming President/CEO of Mission Aviation Fellowship-USA, a position he held for thirteen years until 1998. He is the author of *Riding the Heavens* (Zondervan, 2000) and *On the Wings of the Dawn* (Zondervan, 2001).

Gordon Moyes is superintendent of Australia's largest Christian welfare service, Wesley Mission in Sydney. He has received various awards for his contributions to community welfare and other spheres, culminating in being appointed a Companion of the Order of Australia, Australia's highest national honour, in 2002. He has authored over fifty books and booklets, scripted forty-six documentary films and hosts weekly radio and television programs. He has been married to Beverley since 1959.

David Nicholas, a Baptist pastor, is currently Director of Public Relations at Pacific Hills Christian School, Dural,

New South Wales. He is the editor of *Pacificstreams*, the school's quarterly journal, and has authored many publications including a political biography, *The Pacemaker* (Brolga Books, 1969), and a collection of stories under the title *Musical Wheat* (HarperCollins*Religious*, 1997). He has written for many newspapers and magazines in both Australia and America.

Fred Nile has been a member of the New South Wales Legislative Council for over twenty years. He is well known for his uncompromising commitment to Christian family values. *Fred Nile: An Autobiography* (Strand Publishing, 2001) tells Fred's story and reveals a man who is a fascinating mixture of moral crusader, humble pastor, tireless politician and compassionate human being. He and his wife, Elaine, also a member of the Legislative Council, live in Gerroa, New South Wales.

Brian Pickering is the National Coordinator of the Australian Prayer Network, the largest prayer network in the country, linking some 3200 churches, prayer groups and intercessors. He has an extensive ministry coordinating prayer for the nation and for many years has led prayer outreaches and assignments in different parts of the country, with a major focus on encouraging people to take spiritual responsibility for their communities. He is married with three daughters and two grandchildren. (Australian Prayer Network website: www.ausprayernet.org.au)

Margaret Reeson, together with her husband Ron, worked as missionaries for many years in Papua New Guinea before returning to Australia in 1978. She has since served in a voluntary capacity in local congregations and on several state and federal boards and committees of the Uniting Church. She is currently Moderator of the church's New South Wales synod. She has published eight books in the areas of biography and social history but says her favourite role is as mother and grandmother.

Kel Richards is a Sydney-based author, journalist and broadcaster. He writes and presents 'WordWatch' on ABC NewsRadio, 'Word of the Day' on Clive Robertson's Classic FM Breakfast, and 'Reflection' each week night on 103.2 FM. Kel is author of some twenty-four books, including the best seller *The Case of the Vanishing Corpse* and the recent *Kel Richards' WordWatch* (Pan Macmillan, 2001) and *Jesus On Trial* (Matthias Media, 2001). Kel is married to Barbara and they have two adult children. *Bush Ballads* is his first CD.

Warwick Saxby has been a fitter and machinist, a nursing sister, an owner-operator of a Christian bookshop, a corporate retail manager and a Bible college student. He has been married to Dianne, a chef, for twenty years and they have three teenage children. He is presently an ordained minister with the Assemblies of God and a practising sculptor—and, yes, people do buy his work.

Amanda Smith is a stay-at-home mum and freelance

writer and speaker. She is originally from Brisbane but currently lives in Cincinnati, USA, where she and her husband, James, are involved in ministry at Bridgetown Church of Christ and Cincinnati Bible College and Seminary. They have two young daughters.

Diana Thomas was born in Haifa, Israel, and after immigrating to Australia worked in Western Australia as a registered nurse. In 1993 she went to work with the aid organisation Shelter Now International in Peshawar, Pakistan, as personal assistant to the executive director, at the same time using her nursing skills running a clinic for malnourished children in overcrowded Afghan refugee camps. In 2000 Diana and other Shelter Now personnel moved to the organisation's base in Kabul, Afghanistan. On 5 August 2001 she was arrested and imprisoned by the Taliban, along with seven other Shelter Now workers, for three-and-a-half months.

Irene Voysey is a freelance writer and evangelistic speaker based in Sydney. She was born and educated in India, and later lived in Hong Kong for seventeen years where she wrote a best-seller, *Houseplants for Asian Homes*. In 1989 she won an award from the Australian Religious Press Association for an article on relationships. She was editor of the Bible Society in Australia's magazine, *The Sower*, for ten years and now writes for the Bible League.

Darlene Zschech is the worship pastor of Hillsong Church in Sydney and the co-producer of Hillsong's highly successful praise and worship albums. Known around the world for 'Shout to the Lord' and other worship songs, Darlene has also written a book, *Extravagant Worship* (Bethany House, 2002). She and her husband Mark are executive directors of Mercy Ministries Australia, a non-profit ministry which provides shelter, help and hope to troubled young women. Darlene and Mark have three daughters.

Credits

'Mountain-Moving Faith', © 2002 Gordon Moyes.

'Skin Deep Fear' by Max Meyers is adapted from *Riding the Heavens: Stories and Adventures to Inspire Your Faith* (Grand Rapids: Zondervan Publishing House, 2000), pp. 69–71.

'In the Heart of Afghanistan's Suffering' by Diana Thomas is adapted from *The Voice of the Martyrs* newsletter, March 2002.

'How Much for the Artificial Legs?' by Colin Buchanan. © 2002 Wanaaring Road Music Pty Ltd. All rights reserved.

'Attitude Makes the Difference' by Philip Baker is adapted from *Attitudes of Amazing Achievers* (Perth: Webb & Partners, 2000), pp. 44–45.

'The Little Things', © 2002 Warwick Saxby.

'Miracle in Capernaum' by Geoff Bullock is adapted from *Power of Your Love* (Sydney: Strand Publishing, 2000), pp. 83–87.

'A Tale of Two Pubs' by Michael Frost is from *Alive Magazine*, Dec. 2001/Jan. 2002. Michael writes: 'I am indebted to Sarah Chapman from Scripture Gift Mission for introducing the Cock & Bottle to me through her article "Last Orders" in the SGM magazine, *Interact*.'

'I'm Rich!' by Grenville Kent is adapted from *Signs of the Times*, 4/2001.

'The Power of Praise' by Darlene Zschech is adapted from *Extravagant Worship* (Minneapolis: Bethany House, 2002), pp. 37–39.

'Giving out of Poverty', © 2002 Amanda Smith.

'More Beyond', © 2002 Gordon Moyes.

'Aced by Despair' by Margaret Court and Barbara Oldfield is from *Winning Faith: The Margaret Court Story* (Sydney: Strand Publishing, 2000), pp. 46–56.

'Meeting the Megastar' by John Dickson is adapted from *A Hell of a Life* (Sydney: Matthias Media, 1996).

'September Agent', © 2002 Irene Voysey.

'Fair Dinkum with God', © 2001 Kel Richards. All fourteen of Kel Richards' *Bush Ballads* are available on CD from your local bookshop or direct from the publisher on (02) 9427 4197 or beacon@planet.net.au

'Come Home', © 2002 Brian Pickering.

'Lesson in a Petrol Station', © 2002 Kim Hawtrey.

'Finding God in the Mud', © 2002 Michael Frost.

'The Strangest Gift' by Phillip Jensen is from *Southern Cross*, October 2001.

'Big Plan' by Angela Eynaud is from *Alive Magazine*, April 2002.

'Rita and Evonne' by Dave Andrews is adapted from *Not Religion, But Love* (Oxford: Lion Publishing, 2001).

'Lego and Life', © 2002 Kim Hawtrey.

'Doughnuts' by Philip Baker is adapted from *Attitudes of Amazing Achievers* (Perth: Webb & Partners, 2000), pp. 123–126.

'God As Business Partner', © 2002 Gordon Moyes.

Australian Stories for the Heart

'A Canticle for Catherine', © 2002 Sue Duggan.

'Narrabeen's Story' by Mal Garvin is adapted from 'The Aussie girl who named a beach and showed the spirit of Easter', © 1991 Easter '91.

'The Idol Busyness of Suburbia' by Phillip Jensen is from *Southern Cross*, November 2001.

'Destination: Anywhere' by Colin Buchanan, March 1997. © 1999 Wanaaring Road Music Pty Ltd. All rights reserved.

'The Party Dress' by Angela Eynaud is from *Christian Woman*, May/June 2002.

'Neil's Spiritual U-turn', © 2002 Philip Johnson.

'The Widow's Mite', © 2002 Jonathan Krause.

'Photos, Faith and Finances', © 2002 Steve Grace.

'Doubts' by Max Meyers is adapted from *Riding the Heavens: Stories and Adventures to Inspire Your Faith* (Grand Rapids: Zondervan Publishing House, 2000), pp. 19–25.

'Does God Watch Football?' © 2002 Nathan Brown is adapted from *Signs of the Times*, 8/2001.

'Signposts' by Ken Duncan is from *America Wide: In God We Trust* (Ken Duncan Panographs, 2001).

'The Devil Pushed Me' by Fred Nile is adapted from *Fred Nile: An Autobiography* (Sydney: Strand Publishing, 2001), pp. 1–9.

'A Church with Sole' by Michael Frost is from *Alive Magazine*, July, 2001.

'The Squatter and the Swaggie', © 2001 Kel Richards. All fourteen of Kel Richards' *Bush Ballads* are available on CD from your local bookshop or direct from the publisher on (02) 9427 4197 or beacon@planet.net.au

'Radio Saved Her Life', © 2002 Gordon Moyes.

'Living for Tomorrow', © 2002 Amanda Smith.

'God's Improbable Choices', © 2002 John Mallison.

'A Small Butterfly', © 2002 Margaret Reeson.

'The Unseen Hand', © 2002 Dudley Foord.

'It's Raining Men' by Darlene Zschech is adapted from *Extravagant Worship* (Minneapolis: Bethany House, 2002), pp. 164.

'The Not-Sure Syndrome' by Kim Hawtrey is adapted from *First Impression* (Sydney: Aquila Press, 1994), pp. 17–18.

'The Heart of O'Doherty' by Irene Voysey is adapted from an article first published in *Good News and You*, a publication of the Bible Society in Australia (NSW), June 1991, p. 2.

'Never, Never Give Up', © 2002 Dudley Foord.

'Answers to Prayer', © 2002 Brian Pickering.

'The Gates of Hell' by Geoff Bullock is adapted from *Power of Your Love* (Sydney: Strand Publishing, 2000), pp. 132–136.

'Grace-Filled Living', © 2002 Michael Frost.

'The Real Thing', © 2002 Angela Eynaud.

'The Girl Who Was Always Ahead', © 2002 David R. Nicholas.

'Stranger Than Fiction' by John Dickson is adapted from *A Hell of a Life* (Sydney: Matthias Media, 1996).

'Removing the *Jody V Millennium*', © 2002 Michael Frost.

'No Swimming!' by Ken Duncan is from *Classic Australia* (Ken Duncan Panographs, 2002).

'The Back of Bourke' by Colin Buchanan. © 2002 Wanaaring Road Music Pty Ltd. All rights reserved.

'Breakfast and Blessing' by Darlene Zschech is adapted from *Extravagant Worship* (Minneapolis: Bethany House, 2002), pp. 23–25.

'Overcoming Entropy', © 2002 Amanda Smith.

'The Day Christ Stopped the Bulldozers' by Dave Andrews is adapted from *Not Religion, But Love* (Oxford: Lion Publishing, 2001).

'Hedonists Don't Get No Satisfaction' by Grenville Kent is adapted from *Signs of the Times*, 9/2001.

'The Truth Versus the Facts' by Christine Caine is adapted from *I'm Not Who I Thought I Was* (Castle Hill: Geber Publishing, 2001), pp. 27, 46–49.

'God in the Strip Club', © 2002 Michael Frost.

'My Escape from the World Trade Centre' by Hans Kunnen is adapted from *Signs of the Times*, 8/2002.

'Meeting the Godfather' by Grenville Kent is adapted from *Signs of the Times*, 7/2001.